THE ALOHA ST▪▪▪ ▪▪▪
100 DESTINATIONS YOU MUST VISIT

HAWAII

TRAVEL GUIDE

DIANA L.
MITCHELL

Cover image: © hmmunoz512, Pixabay sourced from canva.com

Table of Contents

Dear reader, thanks a lot for purchasing my book.

To help you plan your trip even more efficiently, I have included an interactive map powered by Google My Maps.

To access it, scan the QR code below.

Happy travelling!

A Note to Our Valued Readers

Thank you for choosing this travel guide as your companion for exploring the world.

I want to take a moment to address a concern you might have regarding the absence of photographs in this book.

As an independent author and publisher, I strive to deliver high-quality, informative content at an affordable price.

Including photographs in a printed book, however, presents significant challenges. Licensing high-quality images can be extremely costly, and unfortunately, I have no control over the print quality of images within the book.

Because these guides are printed and shipped by Amazon, I am unable to review the final print quality before they reach your hands.

So, rather than risk compromising your reading experience with subpar visuals, I've chosen to focus on providing detailed, insightful content that will help you make the most of your travels.

While this guide may not contain photos, it's packed with valuable information, insider tips, and recommendations to ensure you have an enriching and memorable journey.

Additionally, there's an interactive map powered by Google My Maps—an essential tool to help you plan your trip.

I encourage you to supplement your reading with online resources where you can find up-to-date images and visuals of the destinations covered in this guide.

I hope you find this book a helpful and inspiring resource as you embark on your next adventure.

Thank you for your understanding and support.

Safe travels,

Diana

Introduction

Welcome to *Hawaii Travel Guide*, your ultimate resource for exploring the diverse and enchanting destinations across the Hawaiian Islands. From the bustling streets of Honolulu to the serene beaches of Kauai, this guide offers a gateway to the natural beauty, rich history, and unique culture that define Hawaii.

Our journey begins on Oahu, the heart of Hawaii, where urban energy meets natural beauty. Visit The Royal Hawaiian Center and Waikiki Beach for a blend of luxury and leisure. Hike up Diamond Head State Monument for panoramic views, explore the cultural depths at the Shangri La Museum of Islamic Art, Culture & Design, and discover marine wonders at Hanauma Bay Nature Preserve.

Next, we venture to Maui, known for its lush landscapes and stunning coastlines. Witness the sunrise from Haleakala National Park's summit or take the scenic Road to Hana, stopping at Wai'anapanapa State Park. Explore Makawao and Paia towns or relax at Wailea Beach. Maui offers a mix of adventure and relaxation, from Lahaina's historic streets to Kapalua Bay Beach's tranquility.

On the Big Island of Hawaii, volcanic landscapes and diverse ecosystems create dramatic backdrops. Visit Ka Lae and the unique Green Sand Beach at Papakolea. Experience Hawaii Volcanoes National Park's raw power and the tranquility of Rainbow Falls and Akaka Falls State Park. Mauna Kea Summit offers unparalleled stargazing, while the Kona Coffee Living History Farm provides a taste of the island's rich agricultural heritage.

Kauai enchants with lush landscapes and serene beaches. Hike through Waimea Canyon State Park or explore the Na Pali Coast State Wilderness Park. The Kalalau Trail offers unforgettable hiking, while Hanalei Bay and Tunnels Beach are perfect for relaxation. Discover Limahuli Garden and Preserve's botanical beauty and Kilauea Lighthouse's historical charm.

On Molokai, experience a slower pace and deep connection to Hawaiian culture. The Kalaupapa National Historical Park tells the poignant story of the Hansen's disease settlement, while Halawa Valley offers insights into traditional Hawaiian life.

Finally, Lanai offers secluded beaches and rugged landscapes. Explore Polihua Beach and Shipwreck Beach and discover Lanai's heritage at the Lanai Culture & Heritage Center and the Lanai Cat Sanctuary.

Hawaii Travel Guide invites you to experience the diverse beauty, history, and culture of Hawaii. Each destination offers an authentic and memorable journey through the Hawaiian Islands. Pack your bags and get ready to explore Hawaii like never before!

About Hawaii

Landscape of Hawaii

In *Hawaii Travel Guide*, we explore not just the places but the very canvas they are painted upon – the diverse and enchanting landscape of Hawaii. This chapter delves into the varied terrains and natural wonders that make the Aloha State a showcase of the Pacific's natural beauty.

Coastal Charm: Beaches and Coves of the Islands

Hawaii is world-renowned for its scenic coastline. From the iconic surf spots of the North Shore on Oahu to the tranquil shores of Hapuna Beach on the Big Island, the islands' coastlines offer a dramatic meeting of land and sea. The coast is dotted with historic lighthouses, like the Diamond Head Lighthouse, standing as guardians of the islands' rich maritime history. The ocean's influence is evident in the unique culture of these coastal communities, where surfing and fishing traditions continue to flourish.

Urban Green Spaces and Waterfalls

The urban landscapes of Honolulu and Hilo are skillfully interwoven with lush green spaces. The Waikiki Beach Walk and the Liliuokalani Gardens provide serene escapes within the bustling cities. The Manoa Falls in Oahu offers a picturesque backdrop to urban adventures and is a popular spot for hiking and nature walks.

Rolling Hills and Volcanic Landscapes: The Central Highlands

The central regions of the islands, like Maui's Upcountry, are characterized by rolling hills and the dramatic landscapes of volcanic craters such as

Haleakala. These highlands are a patchwork of organic farms, rustic towns, and forested landscapes with sweeping views of the islands below. This heartland is also home to iconic volcanic features and offers a range of outdoor activities, from horseback riding to mountain biking.

The Volcanic Majesty: Hawaii's Big Island

The Big Island is dominated by its volcanic landscapes, including the active eruptions of Kilauea at Hawaii Volcanoes National Park. This region is a haven for nature lovers and outdoor enthusiasts. The park offers a blend of natural attractions set against a backdrop of dramatic volcanic formations and lush rainforests. The highest peak in the Pacific, Mauna Kea, provides breathtaking views and is a popular spot for stargazing and hiking.

The Unique Charm of the Smaller Islands

No description of Hawaii's landscape would be complete without mentioning the smaller islands like Lanai and Molokai. These destinations are characterized by their rugged landscapes, historic sites, and unique ecosystems. Lanai offers a blend of luxury and adventure with its unspoiled terrains, while Molokai remains true to its roots with minimal commercial development, preserving its serene and rustic landscapes.

The Rivers and Waterfalls

Hawaii is also a land of rivers and cascading waterfalls, which play a crucial role in its ecosystem. The Wailuku River on the Big Island, the longest river in Hawaii, features the dramatic Rainbow Falls. The lush vegetation surrounding Hawaii's waterfalls and rivers supports a diverse wildlife and provides numerous opportunities for eco-tourism and adventure.

In Conclusion

The landscape of Hawaii is as diverse as its history and culture. From sandy beaches to volcanic peaks, from bustling urban parks to tranquil waterfalls, the state's natural beauty offers something for every traveler. As you journey through these landscapes, remember that they are not just the backdrop but an integral part of the story of Hawaii.

The Flora and Fauna of Hawaii

In *Hawaii Travel Guide*, we not only traverse through islands and shores but also delve into the rich tapestry of natural life that Hawaii harbors. This chapter is dedicated to exploring the diverse flora and fauna that enrich the landscapes of the Aloha State, offering a glimpse into the vibrant ecosystems that thrive here.

Flora: A Botanical Mosaic

Hawaii's flora is a vibrant mosaic, shaped by its unique geography and climate zones. From the lush tropical rainforests to the volcanic slopes and coastal areas, each ecosystem boasts its own unique plant life.

Coastal Vegetation: Along the Pacific coast, salt-tolerant grasses, coconut palms, and hibiscus dominate. The beaches are often lined with naupaka and beach morning glory.

Forests: The islands are home to diverse forest types. Lowland rainforests contain ohia lehua and koa trees, while the higher altitudes are populated with species like the mamane and the silversword.

Wetlands and Marshes: Wetlands, such as the Kawainui Marsh on Oahu, are crucial for biodiversity. They support various native ferns, sedges, and the unique Hawaiian stilt. These areas are vital for water purification and flood control.

Unique Species: Hawaii is home to numerous endemic plant species due to its isolation, such as the nene (Hawaiian goose), the state bird, and the kukui (candlenut tree), the state tree. The islands also protect several endangered plant species within their borders.

Fauna: From the Forests to the Seas

The animal life in Hawaii is as diverse as its flora, ranging from marine species in the surrounding ocean to various birds, mammals, and insects in inland areas.

Marine Life: The surrounding waters are teeming with life, including various species of dolphins, sea turtles, and fish. The Hawaiian Islands Humpback Whale National Marine Sanctuary is a prime spot for whale watching, where species like the humpback whale are often sighted.

Birds: Hawaii is a haven for birdwatchers. The islands attract unique species such as the Hawaiian honeycreepers, nene, and migratory seabirds like the albatross. Forests and coastal areas provide critical habitat for these birds.

Mammals: Native mammals are mostly limited to marine species, including the Hawaiian monk seal. Introduced species like the wild boar and the mongoose can also be found in forests and rural areas.

Insects and Reptiles: A variety of insects, including the Kamehameha butterfly (state insect), contribute to pollination and the ecological balance. Native reptiles like the Hawaiian green sea turtle are prominent yet protected due to their endangered status.

Preservation and Conservation Efforts

Hawaii is committed to preserving its natural heritage. Various conservation programs and protected areas ensure the survival of many species and their habitats. Efforts like the Hawaiian Islands National Wildlife Refuge protect not only the well-known species but also the lesser-known yet equally important plants and animals.

In Conclusion

The flora and fauna of Hawaii are integral to the state's identity and allure. They add depth and color to the landscape and are essential for the ecological balance. As you explore the destinations in this guide, take a moment to appreciate the natural beauty and biodiversity that Hawaii has to offer. It's not just about the places we visit, but also about the living tapestry that forms the backdrop of our journey.

The Climate of Hawaii

In *Hawaii Travel Guide*, the climate plays a pivotal role in shaping the experiences of each destination. This chapter delves into the climate of Hawaii, offering insights into how it influences the landscapes, flora, fauna, and the overall travel experience across the islands.

Seasonal Variations: A Year-Round Perspective

Hawaii enjoys a tropical climate, marked by only two main seasons which bring about their own unique charm and challenges.

Summer (May to October): This season is generally warmer and drier, with temperatures ranging comfortably in the mid-80s (°F). The weather is ideal for beach activities and exploring the islands' numerous outdoor attractions. Rainfall is less frequent, but passing showers can occur, especially on the windward (eastern) sides of the islands.

Winter (November to April): Winter in Hawaii is slightly cooler and wetter, with temperatures still pleasant in the high 70s to low 80s (°F). This is the season for watching humpback whales, a popular attraction as these majestic creatures migrate to Hawaiian waters. Increased rainfall during this period replenishes the lush landscapes, making them particularly vibrant.

Regional Climate Differences

The climate in Hawaii varies significantly across its islands and even within each island, primarily influenced by elevation and orientation relative to the prevailing trade winds:

Leeward Areas: These areas, typically on the western sides of the islands, experience less rainfall and are generally warmer. Beaches like Waikiki and resorts in Wailea enjoy sunny days almost year-round.

Windward Areas: Located on the eastern sides, these areas receive more rainfall, supporting lush tropical forests and waterfalls. Places like Hilo and the Ko'olau Range are known for their wetter conditions and verdant scenery.

Higher Elevations: Regions at higher altitudes such as Haleakala on Maui or Mauna Kea on the Big Island can be significantly cooler, with temperatures that can drop to near freezing at night. These areas may even experience occasional snowfall in winter.

Impact of Climate Change

Climate change is impacting Hawaii, with rising sea levels threatening coastal areas and warmer ocean temperatures affecting coral reefs. These changes are being closely monitored to understand their long-term effects on Hawaii's natural environment and tourism.

Preparing for Travel

When planning a visit to Hawaii, consider the relatively stable weather conditions:

Summer: Pack lightweight clothing, sunscreen, and a hat for sun protection. Always have water on hand to stay hydrated.

Winter: Light layers are advisable, along with a light jacket for evenings and trips to higher elevations. Rain gear can be useful for visits to windward areas.

In Conclusion

The climate of Hawaii adds to the islands' appeal, offering a dynamic backdrop that remains inviting year-round. Whether you're snorkeling in the crystal-clear Pacific waters, hiking through tropical rainforests, or enjoying the cultural festivities, understanding the climate will enhance your experience and help you prepare for a memorable visit.

The History of Hawaii

In *Hawaii Travel Guide*, the history of Hawaii is not just a backdrop but a vital component of the islands' identity. This chapter takes you on a journey through time, exploring the rich historical tapestry that has shaped Hawaii into the vibrant state it is today.

Indigenous Roots and Kingdom Era

Long before Western contact, Hawaii was inhabited by Polynesian explorers who navigated across vast oceanic expanses, eventually making these islands their home. The indigenous Hawaiian culture flourished, with a complex social system and traditions deeply connected to the land and sea.

The establishment of the Kingdom of Hawaii in 1810 by King Kamehameha the Great marked the unification of the islands under a single ruler. This era was characterized by royal leadership and the codification of laws, contributing significantly to the islands' governance and societal structure.

Colonial Influences and the Overthrow

The arrival of European and American missionaries and traders in the early 19th century introduced new elements to Hawaiian society, including Christianity, commerce, and eventually political change. The missionaries' influence led to significant social and cultural shifts, while traders engaged with the islands' resources.

The late 19th century saw increased political tension and economic interests from the United States, culminating in the overthrow of the Hawaiian monarchy in 1893. Queen Liliʻuokalani was deposed, leading to the eventual annexation of Hawaii by the United States in 1898.

Territorial Period and Statehood

As a U.S. territory from 1900, Hawaii underwent further transformations, including significant military buildup and the introduction of large-scale agriculture, which reshaped the landscape and labor dynamics with the influx of workers from Japan, the Philippines, China, and Portugal.

Hawaii's strategic importance was underscored by the events of December 7, 1941, when the Japanese attack on Pearl Harbor thrust the United States into World War II. Post-war, Hawaii continued to grow economically and culturally, leading to its admission as the 50th state of the United States in 1959.

Cultural Renaissance and Modern Era

The latter half of the 20th century and into the 21st century saw a cultural renaissance, with a revitalization of Hawaiian language, traditions, and arts, emphasizing the importance of heritage and identity.

Today, Hawaii is a unique blend of cultures and histories, with a strong commitment to preserving its Native Hawaiian heritage alongside its modern American state identity.

Historical Landmarks and Legacy

Hawaii is dotted with historical landmarks, from the royal Iolani Palace in Honolulu and the poignant Pearl Harbor National Memorial to the ancient petroglyphs in Puako. These sites offer a window into the past, allowing visitors to step back in time and experience the islands' rich history.

In Conclusion

Understanding the history of Hawaii is crucial to appreciating its present. From its indigenous roots to its royal past, through the transformative events of annexation and statehood, to its ongoing legacy of cultural preservation, Hawaii's history is a testament to the resilience and spirit of its people. As you explore the destinations in this guide, take a moment to reflect on the historical significance of each location, and how it has contributed to the tapestry that is Hawaii today.

Oahu

1.   The Royal Hawaiian Center

The Center's location is historically significant, being part of an area known as Helumoa, which was once the playground of Hawaiian royalty. Today, the Royal Hawaiian Center honors this legacy by providing visitors with an opportunity to engage in cultural learning experiences such as hula lessons, ukulele classes, and Hawaiian quilting, all taught by native experts and free of charge.

Retail offerings at the Center range from luxury brands like Cartier and Rolex to popular global chains such as Apple and Forever 21, catering to all tastes and budgets. The Center also boasts a diverse range of dining options, from fine dining at upscale restaurants like Wolfgang's Steakhouse to quick bites at local food stalls, offering everything from traditional Hawaiian dishes to international cuisine.

The heart of the Royal Hawaiian Center is the Royal Grove, a lushly landscaped garden that pays homage to the area's royal past with native plants and a statue of Princess Bernice Pauahi Bishop, the last royal descendant of the Kamehameha family. The Royal Grove is the centerpiece for cultural performances and events, providing a picturesque setting where visitors can enjoy authentic Hawaiian music and dance under the stars.

Beyond shopping and dining, the Center is deeply involved in the preservation of Hawaiian culture. It hosts regular cultural events that celebrate various aspects of Hawaiian life, from the annual Lei Day celebration to the festive holiday performances. These events are designed to educate both locals and tourists about the rich history and cultural practices of Hawaii.

In conclusion, the Royal Hawaiian Center is more than just a shopping destination. It is a vibrant cultural institution that offers a unique blend of commerce, history, and culture.

2.   Waikiki Beach

Waikiki Beach is one of the most famous beaches in the world, renowned for its long stretch of golden sand and gentle waves, making it perfect for both novice surfers and seasoned sun-seekers. Located on the south shore of Honolulu, this iconic beach is backed by the dramatic Diamond Head crater and flanked by palm trees, luxury hotels, and bustling city streets, creating a picturesque setting that captures the essence of Hawaii.

The history of Waikiki is as rich as its views are stunning. Once a retreat for Hawaiian royalty, Waikiki became popular with international travelers in the early 20th century when the Moana Surfrider, the first hotel in the area, opened its doors in 1901. Since then, Waikiki has evolved into a global hotspot for tourism, combining Hawaiian tradition with modern attractions.

Waikiki is more than just a beach; it is a center of activity where visitors can engage in numerous water sports including surfing, stand-up paddleboarding, and outrigger canoeing. The beach is also a prime location for catamaran cruises and submarine tours that explore the vibrant marine life of the Pacific.

Adjacent to the beach is Kalakaua Avenue, known for its world-class shopping, dining, and entertainment options. Here, visitors can explore international fashion houses, local boutiques, and dine at oceanfront restaurants that offer both gourmet Hawaiian cuisine and dishes from around the world.

As the sun sets, Waikiki becomes even more lively with torch lighting ceremonies, live music, and traditional hula dancing along the beach walk. These nightly performances, coupled with the warm, aloha spirit of the locals, make Waikiki not just a place to visit, but an experience to be cherished.

In essence, Waikiki Beach epitomizes the beauty and culture of Hawaii. It's a place where history, culture, and natural beauty converge to create a vibrant, unforgettable atmosphere. Whether you're here to catch your first wave, enjoy a romantic sunset, or simply relax on the sandy shores, Waikiki offers a slice of Hawaiian paradise that appeals to all.

3.   Diamond Head State Monument

Diamond Head State Monument is one of Hawaii's most distinguished landmarks, known for its historic hiking trail, stunning coastal views, and military history. Formed more than 300,000 years ago during a single explosive eruption, this iconic tuff cone is visible from virtually every part of Honolulu and symbolizes the natural beauty and adventurous spirit of Oahu.

The monument covers over 475 acres, including the interior and outer slopes of the crater. The hike to the summit of Diamond Head is perhaps the most popular activity here. This 0.8-mile hike from the crater floor to the summit is steep and strenuous but offers unparalleled views of Honolulu, Waikiki Beach, and the Pacific Ocean. The trail includes a series of switchbacks, stairs, tunnels, and old military bunkers—an echo of Diamond Head's role as a strategic military lookout in the early 20th century.

The summit provides visitors with a 360-degree view of the lush Oahu coastline and the urban cityscape of Honolulu, making it one of the best spots for photography on the island. Interpretive signs along the trail provide historical context and help hikers understand the geological and military significance of the area.

Diamond Head is not just a popular tourist spot; it's also a State Monument recognized for its historical, cultural, and environmental preservation. Efforts are continually made to maintain the trail, manage the natural habitat, and protect native species that thrive in the unique ecosystem of the crater.

Visiting Diamond Head offers more than just a physical challenge; it's a journey through the natural history of Hawaii, offering insights into the island's volcanic formation and its use throughout the centuries—from ancient Hawaiians who considered it sacred, to its strategic military use in the 1900s, and now as a protected state park. For those looking to capture the essence of Hawaii's natural beauty and historical depth, Diamond Head State Monument stands as a must-visit destination.

4.   Shangri La Museum of Islamic Art, Culture & Design

Nestled against the dramatic backdrop of the Pacific Ocean and Diamond Head, the Shangri La Museum of Islamic Art, Culture & Design stands as a testament to the vision and passion of Doris Duke, an heiress who fell in love with the art and architecture of the Islamic world. Built in the 1930s as a personal retreat and constructed over a span of nearly 60 years, Shangri La houses an extensive collection of Islamic artworks that Duke collected from her travels across North Africa, the Middle East, Central Asia, and South Asia.

Shangri La is more than just a home or museum; it is an immersive experience into Islamic art and culture. The architecture of the building integrates traditional Islamic designs, such as intricate tile work, carved wood, and elaborate mosaics, creating a seamless blend of the various artistic styles and influences from across the Islamic world. The estate itself is a masterpiece, featuring a Syrian mihrab from the 13th century, intricate Moroccan wood carvings, and Persian tiles.

The museum's collection includes approximately 2,500 objects, which range from ceramics and textiles to jewelry and glass, reflecting the rich cultural heritage and artistic achievements of Islamic civilizations. Notably, the museum also focuses on contemporary works, hosting artists in residence, which fosters a dialogue between traditional Islamic art forms and contemporary artistic expressions.

Guided tours of Shangri La not only cover the art collection but also delve into the life of Doris Duke, her travels, her philanthropic endeavors, and her deep appreciation for Islamic culture. These tours offer a narrative that connects the past with the present, highlighting the enduring influence of Islamic art.

Visitors to Shangri La leave with a deeper understanding of Islamic art and architecture, an appreciation of cultural diversity, and inspiration from the beauty and complexity of the Islamic aesthetic. The museum, through its exhibits and programs, continues to educate and inspire, serving as a bridge between cultures and a reminder of the arts' power to unify peoples across different backgrounds.

5.   Hanauma Bay Nature Preserve

Hanauma Bay Nature Preserve, nestled on the southeast coast of Oahu, is one of Hawaii's most famous natural attractions. This stunningly beautiful marine embayment was formed within a tuff ring and is renowned for its vibrant marine ecosystem, making it a top spot for snorkeling and ecological education.

The bay's history as a recreational spot dates back to the 1950s when it became increasingly popular, leading to environmental degradation due to overuse. Recognizing the need to preserve its delicate aquatic ecosystem, Hanauma Bay was designated a protected marine life conservation area and underwater park in 1967. Today, the bay is carefully managed to balance recreational use with environmental preservation.

Visitors to Hanauma Bay are required to watch an educational video before entering the park, highlighting the importance of marine life conservation and how to minimize human impact on the fragile coral reefs. This initiative is part of a broader effort to foster a sustainable relationship between visitors and the natural environment.

The bay's clear, calm waters are ideal for snorkeling, providing up-close encounters with an array of tropical fish, sea turtles, and other marine life. The preserve is home to over 400 species of fish, many of which are endemic to Hawaii. The curved bay and protective reef provide a safe swimming area, making it perfect for families and snorkelers of all skill levels.

The surrounding area features hiking trails and picnic spots, offering spectacular views of the bay and the Pacific Ocean. The educational center on-site provides further insights into the marine life and ecosystems of Hawaii, enhancing visitor understanding and appreciation of the bay's natural heritage.

Hanauma Bay is not only a place for recreation but also an exemplar of environmental stewardship. By limiting the number of visitors per day and enforcing strict guidelines on interaction with the marine environment, the preserve ensures that this natural treasure will continue to thrive and enchant visitors for generations to come.

6.   Koko Crater Railway Trailhead

Koko Crater Railway Trailhead offers one of the most challenging and rewarding hikes in Honolulu, located on the eastern side of Oahu. The trail itself is unique, as it consists of 1,048 railroad ties that ascend the steep slope of Koko Crater. Originally installed during World War II for military access to a lookout post and radar installation, these tracks now serve as a strenuous stairway that attracts fitness enthusiasts and adventurers alike.

The climb to the top of Koko Crater is intense and unforgiving, with no shade and a near-vertical incline in parts. However, the reward for those who reach the summit is unparalleled: panoramic views of the eastern coastline of Oahu, including Hanauma Bay, Diamond Head, and the vast Pacific Ocean. The trail is especially popular at sunrise when the early morning light bathes the island in a soft glow, making the physical challenge all the more worthwhile.

The environment around Koko Crater is rugged yet fragile, with dryland vegetation and small patches of forest that provide habitat for various bird species. Conservation efforts are in place to protect this delicate ecosystem from the impacts of heavy foot traffic.

For those seeking an alternative experience, the backside of Koko Crater offers a less traveled path that leads through botanical gardens and provides a different perspective on the natural beauty of the area. Regardless of the route, hikers are advised to bring water, wear sunscreen, and be prepared for a physically demanding journey.

Koko Crater Railway Trailhead is not just a hiking destination; it's a testament to the resilience of those who tackle its heights and a symbol of the adventurous spirit that defines the Hawaiian experience.

7.   Makapu'u Point Lighthouse Trail

Makapu'u Point Lighthouse Trail, located on the eastern tip of Oahu, offers one of the most scenic hikes in Hawaii. This relatively easy trail provides stunning views of the southeastern coastline, including Koko Head and the distant islands of Molokai and Lanai. The trail is fully paved, making it accessible to walkers of all ages and fitness levels, including those with strollers or wheelchairs.

The highlight of the trail is the historic Makapu'u Lighthouse, built in 1909, which features a distinctive red roof and one of the largest lighthouse lenses in the world. While the lighthouse itself is not open to the public, the trail offers several lookouts where hikers can pause to take in the breathtaking views and possibly spot migrating humpback whales during the winter months.

The area around the trail is a state wildlife sanctuary and is home to native plants and birds. Interpretive signs along the path offer insights into the natural and cultural history of the area, enhancing the educational value of the hike.

The trail culminates at a summit lookout, providing expansive views of the Windward Coast and offshore islets. It's a popular spot for photography, whale watching, or simply enjoying the serene beauty of the Pacific.

8.   Sea Life Park Hawaii

Sea Life Park Hawaii, located on the windward coast of Oahu near Makapu'u Point, offers visitors a unique opportunity to interact with marine life in a spectacular natural setting. The park features a series of aquariums, marine mammal shows, and hands-on experiences that educate and entertain visitors of all ages.

One of the park's main attractions is the dolphin programs, where guests can swim with dolphins, learn about their behaviors, and even participate in a dolphin trainer experience. Similarly, programs with sea lions and rays offer additional opportunities for up-close encounters with marine animals.

The park also conducts important research and conservation work, particularly with native Hawaiian marine species. The Hawaiian Reef Aquarium showcases the vibrant coral life found in local waters, and the park's efforts in sea turtle conservation are highlighted through educational displays and encounters.

Sea Life Park's bird sanctuary is another highlight, where visitors can meet indigenous birds and learn about local conservation efforts. The park's setting, with panoramic views of the Pacific Ocean, enhances the experience, making it not just an educational visit but also a visually stunning one.

By combining fun with education, Sea Life Park Hawaii plays a crucial role in fostering marine conservation awareness, offering a deeper understanding of the ocean's ecosystems and the importance of preserving them for future generations.

9.   Lanikai Beach

Lanikai Beach, situated on the windward coast of Oahu, is often ranked among the best beaches in the world. With its powdery white sand, clear turquoise waters, and the picturesque backdrop of the Mokulua Islands, Lanikai offers a slice of paradise that epitomizes the tropical beauty of Hawaii.

The name "Lanikai" translates to "heavenly sea," a fitting description for this half-mile stretch of coastal bliss. The beach is protected by a nearby coral reef, which ensures calm and serene waters ideal for swimming, snorkeling, and kayaking. The gentle waves and absence of strong currents make Lanikai an excellent choice for families with children or for those seeking a relaxed day by the sea.

One of the unique features of Lanikai Beach is the view of the Mokulua Islands, two islets off the coast that are accessible by kayak. These islands, especially the larger one, Moku Nui, offer adventurous visitors the chance to explore secluded coves and tide pools. Kayaking to these islands provides a fantastic opportunity for wildlife viewing, including sea turtles and various seabirds.

The beauty of Lanikai extends beyond its waters. The beach is framed by a neighborhood of luxurious homes and lush vegetation, which, while limiting public access points to the beach, adds to its exclusive and private feel. There are no public facilities or lifeguards at Lanikai, preserving its unspoiled charm but requiring visitors to come prepared.

For those looking to capture the perfect sunrise in Hawaii, Lanikai Beach is the place to be. The east-facing beach offers spectacular sunrise views that illuminate the Mokulua Islands and the ocean in hues of orange and pink, providing a breathtaking experience and exceptional photography opportunities.

In conclusion, Lanikai Beach is not just a beach but a destination offering tranquility, natural beauty, and a chance to engage in leisurely water activities or simply soak up the sun on its pristine sands. Its reputation as a heavenly spot is well-earned, making it a must-visit for anyone traveling to Oahu.

10.   Kailua Town

Kailua Town, located on the windward side of Oahu, is a charming residential and commercial area known for its laid-back atmosphere and strong sense of community. Unlike the more tourist-centric areas of Honolulu and Waikiki, Kailua offers a glimpse into the everyday life of its residents, coupled with access to some of the island's most stunning natural attractions.

The town features a vibrant mix of local boutiques, unique eateries, and artisanal shops that reflect the eclectic tastes and spirit of its population. Shopping in Kailua Town is a delight, with options ranging from fashionable clothing stores to shops specializing in local crafts and artwork. The weekly Kailua Farmers' Market is a focal point for both locals and visitors, offering fresh local produce, specialty foods, and handmade goods.

Dining in Kailua is similarly diverse, with restaurants serving everything from traditional Hawaiian dishes to international cuisine. Popular spots like Cinnamon's Restaurant offer iconic Hawaiian breakfasts, while Buzz's Original Steak House provides a perfect setting for a beachside meal.

Kailua is also known for its outdoor lifestyle. The nearby Kailua Beach and Lanikai Beach are famous for their beauty, and the town itself has several parks and recreational areas. Adventurers can explore the Pillbox Hike, which provides panoramic views of the Windward coast, or kayak to the Mokulua Islands, a popular day trip.

Culturally, Kailua is a hub for environmental and community-focused initiatives, with numerous organizations dedicated to preserving the area's natural beauty and promoting sustainable living. This community ethos is palpable as you walk the streets, adding to the town's welcoming vibe.

Kailua Town encapsulates the essence of Hawaii's diverse charm, combining natural beauty, cultural richness, and a warm community spirit, making it an essential visit for those looking to experience a more relaxed and authentic side of Hawaiian life.

11.   Kailua Beach

Kailua Beach, located on the windward side of Oahu, is celebrated for its soft white sands, brilliant turquoise waters, and frequent sightings of the Mokulua Islands just offshore. This 2.5-mile long beach is a favorite among both locals and visitors for its excellent conditions for a variety of water sports, including windsurfing, kayaking, and swimming.

The beach's gentle waves and steady wind make it an ideal location for windsurfing and kiteboarding. The shorebreak is generally mild, making it safe for swimmers of all ages, and the clear, shallow waters near the shoreline are perfect for families with children. Kayakers often take to the water to explore the nearby Mokulua Islands, which are visible from the beach and accessible to those looking for a bit more adventure.

Kailua Beach is also known for its scenic beauty and is often less crowded than its famous counterpart, Waikiki Beach. The beach is backed by large ironwood trees that provide ample shade for picnicking or simply enjoying a break from the sun. There are several picnic areas, volleyball courts, and shower facilities available for public use, making it well-equipped for full-day outings.

Each morning, the beach is a popular spot for joggers and walkers who take advantage of the long stretches of sand to exercise with a view. The sunrise over Kailua Beach is particularly breathtaking and is a not-to-be-missed experience for early risers.

The beach's proximity to Kailua Town means that food and amenities are never far away. Local eateries offer everything from quick snacks to gourmet meals, ideal for beachgoers looking to refuel after a day in the sun and sea.

Kailua Beach not only offers a plethora of recreational activities but also stands out as a natural beauty spot that embodies the idyllic Hawaiian beach experience. Its combination of accessibility, beauty, and community atmosphere makes it a standout destination on the island of Oahu.

12.   Kawainui Marsh

Kawainui Marsh is the largest wetland in Hawaii, located in Kailua on the island of Oahu. This 830-acre conservation area is a vital environmental resource and a cherished historical site, playing a significant role in Hawaiian culture and the biodiversity of the region.

Historically, Kawainui Marsh was an important fishpond and agricultural site for Native Hawaiians. Today, it serves as a critical habitat for endangered water birds and a variety of migratory bird species, making it a popular spot for bird watching and environmental studies. The marsh supports species such as the Hawaiian stilt, the Hawaiian coot, and the Hawaiian duck, all of which are endemic to the islands and rely on the wetland for survival.

The area around Kawainui Marsh includes walking trails that allow visitors to explore the wetland and its surroundings. These trails offer educational signage that provides insights into the ecological significance and the restoration efforts that are ongoing to preserve this unique environment. The marsh not only serves as a natural filter improving water quality but also acts as a flood control basin protecting the surrounding community.

Community involvement is key to the preservation efforts at Kawainui Marsh. Local groups frequently organize clean-ups, educational programs, and restoration projects to maintain the health of the marsh and ensure its survival for future generations. These activities offer visitors and volunteers the opportunity to contribute to environmental conservation efforts and learn about the importance of wetlands.

Moreover, the spiritual and cultural significance of Kawainui Marsh adds another layer of depth to its conservation. It is considered a sacred site in Hawaiian culture, historically used for aquaculture and as a place of refuge in times of war.

Kawainui Marsh represents a blend of natural beauty, cultural heritage, and environmental significance. It offers a serene escape from the more developed parts of the island and provides a unique opportunity to engage with Hawaii's natural and cultural history in a meaningful way. Whether you are a bird watcher, a nature lover, or someone interested in the cultural history of Hawaii, Kawainui Marsh offers a rich and rewarding experience.

13.   Byodo-In Temple

Nestled at the foot of the Ko'olau Mountains in Oahu's Valley of the Temples Memorial Park, the Byodo-In Temple stands as a serene and majestic site. This non-denominational temple, which was established in 1968 to commemorate the 100-year anniversary of the first Japanese immigrants to Hawaii, is a scale replica of the over 950-year-old Byodo-In Temple in Uji, Japan.

The Byodo-In Temple in Hawaii is crafted entirely without the use of nails and is a stunning example of traditional Japanese architecture. It features a large Amida Buddha statue, one of the largest carved figures outside of Japan, standing over nine feet tall and made entirely from gold-lacquered wood. The temple is surrounded by lush gardens that include small koi ponds, meditation niches, and walking paths that invite visitors to explore and reflect in the peaceful surroundings.

One of the temple's most distinctive features is its large, hanging brass Peace Bell, housed in a softwood structure near the entrance. Visitors are encouraged to ring the bell for happiness, longevity, and a blessing of tranquility. The sound of the bell, set against the backdrop of the mountains and lush vegetation, creates an atmosphere of profound peace and spiritual relaxation.

The temple and its gardens are a popular site for both tourists and locals looking for a place of peace and beauty. It is also a favored location for weddings and ceremonies due to its picturesque setting and the awe-inspiring architecture of the temple.

Byodo-In Temple serves not only as a place of worship and meditation but also as a bridge between cultures, celebrating the harmony and understanding between the Japanese and Hawaiian people. It stands as a testament to beauty, peace, and the melting pot of cultures that define Hawaii, making it a must-visit destination for those seeking tranquility and a deeper understanding of spiritual and cultural integration.

14.   Kaneohe Sandbar

The Kaneohe Sandbar, located in the middle of Kaneohe Bay on the windward coast of Oahu, is a natural marvel that appears to rise from the middle of the ocean at low tide. This large, natural sandbar is accessible only by boat, kayak, or other watercraft, making it an exclusive and somewhat adventurous destination.

The sandbar's water varies from ankle-deep to waist-high depending on the tide, providing a perfect setting for a day of swimming, snorkeling, and sunbathing in the middle of the bay. The surrounding waters are crystal clear and home to various marine life, offering excellent conditions for snorkeling. The backdrop of the lush Ko'olau Mountains and the azure Pacific Ocean makes the sandbar one of the most scenic spots in Hawaii.

Visitors to the Kaneohe Sandbar can enjoy the unique experience of playing beach volleyball, having a picnic, or simply relaxing on their own slice of sandy paradise in the middle of the bay. The area is also a popular spot for kitesurfing and windsurfing when the conditions are right.

Local tour operators offer trips to the sandbar, providing safety equipment and guidance to ensure a safe and enjoyable experience. These excursions often include BBQs and guided snorkeling tours around the sandbar's perimeter reefs.

The Kaneohe Sandbar is a testament to Oahu's natural beauty and unique geological formations. It provides a rare opportunity to enjoy a beach day far from the shore's edge, surrounded only by water, sky, and the picturesque mountain range. It is truly one of Oahu's hidden gems, offering a memorable and picturesque escape from the hustle and bustle of city life.

15.   Kualoa Ranch

Kualoa Ranch, located on the northeastern side of Oahu, is a 4,000-acre private nature reserve and working cattle ranch that offers a wide range of outdoor activities set against some of Hawaii's most stunning landscapes. The ranch has gained fame not only for its scenic beauty but also as a filming location for numerous Hollywood movies and TV shows, including "Jurassic Park," "Lost," and "Hawaii Five-0."

Visitors to Kualoa Ranch can choose from a variety of tours and activities, including horseback riding, ATV tours, zip-lining, and guided hikes. These tours offer breathtaking views of the ranch's dramatic cliffs, lush valleys, and tropical forests, as well as insights into the area's rich history and cultural significance in native Hawaiian culture.

The ranch also offers unique experiences such as the "Hollywood Movie Sites Tour," which takes visitors to famous filming locations across the property. The "Jurassic Adventure Tour" is particularly popular, allowing guests to explore locations from the Jurassic movie franchise and learn about the ranch's history and natural ecosystems.

Kualoa Ranch is committed to land conservation and sustainability. It conducts educational programs and eco-tours that emphasize the importance of preserving Hawaii's natural landscapes and cultural heritage.

16. Polynesian Cultural Center

The Polynesian Cultural Center, located on Oahu's North Shore, is a cultural theme park and living museum that offers an immersive experience into the cultures of Polynesia. Covering eight simulated tropical villages, the center showcases the traditions, history, and hospitality of six Pacific cultures: Samoa, Aotearoa (New Zealand), Fiji, Hawaii, Tahiti, and Tonga.

Visitors can participate in a variety of hands-on activities and demonstrations, including Samoan cooking, Tahitian dance, Hawaiian games, and Maori tattooing. Each village offers a unique glimpse into the way of life of each culture, presented by natives from each island, providing authentic and engaging educational experiences.

The Polynesian Cultural Center is also known for its spectacular evening show, "HA: Breath of Life," which features over 100 performers in a compelling story of passion, fire, and ritual. The show combines traditional Polynesian dance with modern effects and storytelling techniques.

The center also features a marketplace that sells traditional crafts, clothing, and art from across Polynesia. Dining options include a buffet with a variety of Polynesian dishes, allowing guests to taste the flavors of the islands.

The Polynesian Cultural Center not only entertains but also serves as an important educational resource, preserving and perpetuating the cultures of the Pacific. It is one of Hawaii's most popular attractions, drawing visitors from around the world who leave with a deeper appreciation and understanding of the rich cultural heritage of Polynesia.

17. Sunset Beach

Sunset Beach, located on the North Shore of Oahu, Hawaii, is one of the world's most renowned surf spots, famous for its beautiful sunsets and powerful waves. This spectacular beach stretches for two miles from Ehukai Beach to Velzyland, offering dramatic ocean views and a perfect setting for relaxation and adventure.

During the winter months, Sunset Beach becomes a hub for professional surfers and enthusiasts from around the globe as it hosts prestigious surfing competitions like the Vans Triple Crown of Surfing. The waves here can swell up to thirty feet, creating thrilling rides and spectacular spills that are a marvel to watch. Due to the high surf, winter at Sunset Beach is recommended for experienced surfers and spectators rather than casual swimmers.

Conversely, during the summer months, the sea calms considerably, transforming the beach into a tranquil spot ideal for swimming, snorkeling, and sunbathing. The clearer waters allow for excellent visibility, making it a fantastic time for underwater exploration.

Sunset Beach is also famed for its breathtaking sunsets, which paint the sky in shades of orange, pink, and purple as the sun dips below the horizon. This natural spectacle draws visitors and locals alike, who gather to watch the day end in spectacular fashion.

Beyond the beach, the surrounding area of Sunset Beach offers a laid-back, local vibe with charming cafes, food trucks, and art galleries that showcase the work of local artists. The community here is tightly-knit and exudes a warm, welcoming atmosphere that invites visitors to slow down and savor the island life.

For those looking to explore the natural beauty of Oahu's North Shore, Sunset Beach provides not just a destination, but an experience filled with awe-inspiring views, world-class surfing, and magical sunsets, making it a must-visit for anyone traveling to Hawaii.

18.   Waimea Valley

Nestled in the heart of Oahu's North Shore, Waimea Valley is a historical nature sanctuary that offers a unique blend of Hawaii's natural beauty and cultural heritage. This lush, 1,875-acre park is not only home to stunning botanical gardens but also an important cultural site with significant historical relevance to the Hawaiian people.

Waimea Valley has been a sacred place for more than 700 years, historically used by Hawaiian priests (kahunas) and their apprentices. This valley is rich with archaeological sites, including ancient temples (heiaus) and residential sites, which provide insight into the early Hawaiian civilization.

Visitors to Waimea Valley can explore over 5,000 species of tropical and subtropical plants in its world-class botanical gardens, including rare and endangered species. The gardens are organized into 35 themed collections, such as the Hawaiian Ethnobotanical Garden, which focuses on plants important to Hawaiian cultural practices.

One of the highlights of a visit to Waimea Valley is the Waimea Falls, a beautiful waterfall that cascades into a large pool below. This spot is not only picturesque but also allows for swimming, offering a refreshing dip surrounded by the lush tropical landscape.

Waimea Valley also offers a variety of cultural experiences designed to educate and engage visitors. These include traditional Hawaiian games, crafts, music, and hula performances. The park also hosts guided walks and educational talks that delve into the valley's ecology and archaeological significance.

The preservation efforts in Waimea Valley are robust, with ongoing projects to restore and maintain its historical sites and natural habitats. This beautiful valley offers a peaceful retreat and an educational experience that highlights the natural and cultural heritage of Hawaii, making it a compelling visit for nature lovers and history enthusiasts alike.

19. Laniakea Beach

Laniakea Beach, more commonly known as Turtle Beach, is located on the North Shore of Oahu. This beach is renowned for its frequent sightings of Hawaiian green sea turtles, which often come ashore to bask in the sun. This unique phenomenon provides an incredible opportunity for visitors to observe these majestic creatures up close in their natural habitat.

The beach itself is relatively small and rocky, but the real attraction is the turtles. Conservationists are often on site to monitor and protect the turtles, providing educational talks to visitors about the biology and conservation status of these animals. The presence of the turtles at Laniakea has made it one of the most popular wildlife viewing areas on Oahu.

Visitors to Laniakea Beach are urged to respect the wildlife by keeping a safe distance from the turtles and not attempting to touch them. This respect for nature not only ensures the safety of the turtles but also contributes to the ongoing efforts to protect this endangered species.

Beyond turtle watching, Laniakea Beach offers stunning views of the ocean and the North Shore coastline. The surf here can be strong, and the currents are often powerful, so swimming is usually recommended only for the experienced. The beach is also a popular spot for snorkeling when the water is calm, providing a glimpse into the vibrant marine life that thrives just off the shore.

20.   North Shore

The North Shore of Oahu is legendary, known worldwide as a surfing mecca because of its massive winter waves and professional surfing competitions. Stretching from Ka'ena Point in the west to eastward past Haleiwa town, the North Shore offers more than just spectacular surfing; it embodies a laid-back lifestyle and is steeped in natural beauty.

During the winter months, the North Shore's beaches, including famous spots like Waimea Bay, Banzai Pipeline, and Sunset Beach, come alive with some of the highest waves seen anywhere in the world, attracting surfers and spectators from across the globe. The surfing culture is deeply embedded here, and a visit during this season offers a firsthand look at the sport at its most extreme.

In contrast, the summer months on the North Shore transform the beaches into serene, beautiful spots ideal for swimming, snorkeling, and enjoying the sandy beaches. The calmer waters allow for activities like paddle boarding and kayaking, making it a perfect time for families to visit.

The town of Haleiwa, with its historic buildings, local art galleries, boutiques, and casual dining spots, serves as the cultural hub of the North Shore. This small town offers a glimpse into Hawaii's past with its preserved architecture and relaxed atmosphere.

The North Shore is not just about beautiful beaches and surfing; it's about a lifestyle that celebrates simplicity, nature, and the spirit of Aloha. It remains one of the most authentic and captivating areas of Hawaii, offering a blend of adventure, culture, and natural beauty that is unmatched.

Each of these destinations provides a unique perspective on the diverse beauty and cultural heritage of Hawaii, from serene beaches and historic valleys to the vibrant life of the North Shore. Whether you're looking for adventure, relaxation, or a deep dive into Hawaii's rich history, these places promise memorable experiences that encapsulate the spirit of the islands.

21.   Dole Plantation

Dole Plantation, located in central Oahu, offers a unique glimpse into the history of pineapple cultivation in Hawaii. Once a fruit stand in the 1950s, it has evolved into one of Oahu's most popular attractions, drawing over one million visitors annually. The plantation serves as a tribute to the island's agricultural heritage and provides educational experiences that celebrate Hawaii's pineapple industry.

Spanning 20 acres, Dole Plantation features several attractions designed to educate and entertain. The Pineapple Express Train Ride is a 20-minute journey through the plantation's fields, where visitors learn about the history of pineapple and agriculture in Hawaii through narration. The ride provides a panoramic view of the various crops grown on the plantation, including coffee, cacao, and, of course, pineapples.

Another highlight is the Pineapple Garden Maze, recognized as one of the world's largest mazes. Covering over three acres, the maze is constructed from 14,000 colorful Hawaiian plants and challenges visitors to find secret stations that complete a mystery game. It's both fun and educational for all ages, providing a hands-on learning experience about Hawaiian flora.

The Plantation Garden Tour is a self-guided walk through eight mini-gardens that showcase different varieties of pineapples from around the world and other crops important to Hawaii's agricultural industry. This educational tour offers insight into the botany of pineapples and the diversity of tropical plants.

No visit to Dole Plantation is complete without stopping at the Plantation Country Store, where visitors can purchase Dole's famous pineapple soft serve ice cream, along with a variety of pineapple-themed gifts and local Hawaiian products. The store also features educational displays about the history of Dole and the impact of pineapples on Hawaiian culture and economy.

Dole Plantation not only provides a fun day out for families and visitors of all ages but also plays an important role in preserving and presenting the agricultural history of Hawaii.

22.   Ko Olina Lagoons

Ko Olina Lagoons, located on the west coast of Oahu, are a series of four man-made lagoons that offer idyllic swimming and sunbathing conditions. Known for their crescent-shaped, white-sand beaches and calm, crystal-clear waters, the lagoons provide a perfect retreat for families and those seeking a more secluded beach experience away from the busier tourist spots.

The lagoons, named Kolola, Hanu, Naiʻa, and Ulua, are part of the 642-acre Ko Olina Resort, which includes luxury hotels, vacation rentals, and private residences. Each lagoon has public access and offers ample amenities, including restrooms, showers, and limited parking. The rock barriers that protect the lagoons create tranquil waters ideal for swimming and snorkeling, safe even for young children.

Aside from water activities, the lagoons are surrounded by lush greenery and walking paths that connect all four lagoons. These paths are perfect for jogging, strolling, or enjoying the stunning ocean views, especially during sunset. The area is meticulously maintained, reflecting the resort's high standards and dedication to providing a serene environment.

Ko Olina Lagoons are not just popular with tourists but are also a favored location for weddings and events, thanks to their picturesque settings. The nearby Ko Olina Golf Club and marina offer additional recreational options, including fishing tours and catamaran cruises, making it a comprehensive destination that caters to a variety of interests.

In essence, Ko Olina Lagoons epitomize the beauty and tranquility of Hawaii's landscapes, offering a luxurious and peaceful beach experience. Whether you are looking for a quiet day by the sea, a safe place for family fun, or a scenic jogging route, Ko Olina Lagoons provide a little piece of paradise for everyone.

23.   USS Arizona Memorial

The USS Arizona Memorial at Pearl Harbor in Honolulu, Hawaii, stands as a solemn tribute to the 1,177 crewmen who lost their lives during the Japanese attack on Pearl Harbor on December 7, 1941. This tragic event marked a pivotal moment in U.S. history, drawing the country into World War II. Today, the memorial is visited by more than one million people each year who come to pay their respects and reflect on the impact of war.

The memorial is accessible only by boat. It spans the mid-portion of the sunken USS Arizona battleship without touching it, preserving the sanctity of the tomb. The structure's design is iconic, featuring a sagging center to represent the initial defeat of the attack and its rises at both ends signify American victory and resilience.

Visitors to the memorial begin their experience at the Pearl Harbor Visitor Center, where they can explore extensive exhibits that provide historical context about the Pearl Harbor attack, the events leading up to it, and its aftermath. The exhibits also cover personal stories of those who were involved in the battle, giving a human face to the history.

From there, guests are taken on a short boat ride by the U.S. Navy to the actual memorial. Once at the memorial, visitors can observe the oil that still leaks from the wreckage, known poignantly as the "Tears of the Arizona." Inside, the Shrine Room lists the names of all those who died on the USS Arizona, etched into a marble wall, a poignant reminder of the human cost of war.

The visit to the USS Arizona Memorial is a powerful and moving experience, serving not only as a reminder of those who made the ultimate sacrifice but also as an educational experience that underscores the importance of peace and the harsh realities of conflict.

24. Pearl Harbor National Memorial

The Pearl Harbor National Memorial is a historic site that encompasses several key locations related to the Japanese attack on Pearl Harbor on December 7, 1941. This site serves as a place of remembrance for the lives lost in the attack that precipitated the United States' entry into World War II. Managed by the National Park Service, it aims to educate visitors about the events of that day and the broader war effort, honoring both military and civilian sacrifices.

USS Bowfin Submarine Museum & Park: Nicknamed the "Pearl Harbor Avenger," the USS Bowfin played a significant role in the Pacific during World War II. Visitors can tour the submarine itself, getting a firsthand look at the cramped conditions under which submariners lived and worked. The adjacent museum contains a vast collection of submarine-related artifacts and exhibits.

Battleship Missouri Memorial: Situated where World War II ended with the Japanese surrender in Tokyo Bay, the USS Missouri offers a historic counterpoint to the beginning of the U.S. involvement in the war at Pearl Harbor. The battleship is open for tours, and visitors can stand on the Surrender Deck where the surrender documents were signed, effectively ending World War II.

Pearl Harbor Aviation Museum: Located on Ford Island, this museum is housed in two World War II-era hangars that survived the 1941 attack. The museum showcases an impressive collection of vintage aircraft, including a Japanese Zero and a B-17 Flying Fortress, alongside interactive exhibits that cover aviation's role in the Pacific Theater.

In addition to these attractions, the Pearl Harbor Visitor Center itself offers numerous exhibitions that delve into the historical context of the attack, the political climate of the time, and personal stories from those who lived through the events. The center also provides a sobering overview of the attack with artifacts, photographs, and multimedia presentations that help visitors understand the scale and impact of that day.

25.   Bishop Museum

Bishop Museum, located in Honolulu, Hawaii, is the largest museum in the state and a renowned repository of Polynesian culture and history. Founded in 1889 by Charles Reed Bishop in memory of his late wife, Princess Bernice Pauahi Bishop, the last descendant of the royal Kamehameha family, the museum has grown into an educational center that houses millions of artifacts, documents, and photographs about Hawaii and other Pacific island cultures.

The museum's extensive collections are housed in several buildings on its expansive campus. The Hawaiian Hall and Polynesian Hall are perhaps the most famous, where visitors can explore three floors of exhibits dedicated to the history, culture, and arts of Hawaii and other Pacific islands. These exhibits include an impressive array of Native Hawaiian artifacts, such as feather cloaks, wooden carvings, and traditional weapons, which tell the story of the islands' inhabitants and their ingenious practices and navigational skills.

The Bishop Museum also boasts the Richard T. Mamiya Science Adventure Center, which provides an interactive experience focused on Hawaii's natural history, including volcanology, oceanography, and biodiversity. One of the highlights here is a walk-in volcano that simulates the experience of witnessing a volcanic eruption, complete with rumbling and a lava flow.

Another significant feature of the museum is the Jhamandas Watumull Planetarium, which offers shows that not only explore the stars but also delve into Polynesian navigational techniques using the stars, winds, and waves—skills that were critical to their voyaging across the vast Pacific Ocean.

The Bishop Museum continually updates its exhibits and offers temporary exhibitions, workshops, and educational programs that make it a dynamic place where visitors of all ages can learn about the rich heritage of the Pacific and see how the past connects with contemporary Hawaiian culture. This makes it an invaluable resource for both locals looking to connect with their heritage and tourists eager to learn about the rich cultural tapestry of Hawaii.

26.   Chinatown Historic District

Honolulu's Chinatown Historic District is one of the oldest and most vibrant Chinatowns in the United States. Located in downtown Honolulu, this neighborhood offers a rich tapestry of history, culture, and cuisine. Originally established in the 19th century by Chinese laborers who came to work on Hawaii's sugar plantations, today's Chinatown is a lively blend of Southeast Asian cultures, including Chinese, Japanese, Filipino, and Vietnamese influences.

The area is renowned for its historical architecture, with many buildings dating back to the 1900s. These include the historic Wo Fat Building, the oldest existing restaurant building in Chinatown, and the beautifully restored Hawaii Theatre, a 1920s-era theater that now hosts concerts, lectures, and film festivals. Walking tours of Chinatown give visitors a deeper insight into the architectural and cultural history of the area.

Chinatown is also a culinary destination with a plethora of markets, noodle shops, and restaurants offering authentic Asian cuisines. The Oahu Market, founded in 1904, is a must-visit for food enthusiasts looking to explore local produce and exotic ingredients. The area's vibrant food scene ranges from traditional dim sum and pho to innovative fusion restaurants.

Art and culture thrive in Chinatown, with numerous galleries and boutiques showcasing local artists and designers. The First Friday Art Walk, held on the first Friday of each month, features street festivals and open galleries, drawing a lively crowd.

Chinatown's dynamic blend of historic significance, cultural diversity, and artistic vitality makes it a unique and fascinating part of Honolulu, offering visitors an immersive experience into the heart of the city's multicultural heritage.

27.   Manoa Falls

Manoa Falls is a stunning 150-foot waterfall located in the lush Manoa Valley, just a short drive from downtown Honolulu. This natural attraction is part of the larger Manoa Falls Trail, a 1.6-mile round-trip hike that is considered one of Oahu's most popular hiking destinations due to its scenic views and relative ease.

The trail to Manoa Falls takes hikers through a verdant tropical rainforest, rich with a variety of native Hawaiian plants and bird species, along with historical features such as old terraces from when the area was farmed by Native Hawaiians. The path can be muddy and slippery, but it is well-maintained and suitable for hikers of all skill levels.

Reaching the waterfall, visitors are greeted by the spectacular sight of water cascading down a moss-covered cliff into a small pool below. Swimming is not recommended due to the risk of falling rocks and the presence of harmful bacteria in the water, but the site provides a perfect backdrop for photography and a peaceful spot to enjoy the sounds and sights of nature.

Manoa Falls and its surrounding area are not only a haven for nature lovers but also serve as a living classroom for environmental education, emphasizing the importance of conservation and the protection of Hawaii's natural resources.

28.   Iolani Palace

Iolani Palace in Honolulu stands as a national historic landmark and the only official royal residence in the United States. Built in 1882 by King Kalakaua, this opulent palace was the home of Hawaii's last reigning monarchs and served as the capitol until the overthrow of the Hawaiian Kingdom in 1893. Today, it is a museum open to the public, offering a glimpse into the grandeur of the Hawaiian monarchy.

Visitors to Iolani Palace can tour the beautifully restored rooms, including the throne room, state dining room, and private suites of the royal family, all of which feature original furnishings and artifacts. The palace also displays an array of royal regalia, personal items, and gifts from dignitaries around the world, illustrating the global connections and influence of the Hawaiian monarchy.

Guided tours of the palace are available, providing historical context and stories about the palace's construction, its significance in Hawaiian history, and the lives of the royals who lived there. Additionally, the palace grounds and the Coronation Pavilion are popular sites, offering more insights into the cultural and political history of Hawaii.

Iolani Palace is not just a monument to the past; it is a symbol of the Hawaiian people's pride and resilience. It plays a crucial role in preserving Native Hawaiian culture and history, making it an essential visit for anyone interested in understanding Hawaii's royal heritage and its lasting impact on the islands today.

29.   Honolulu Museum of Art

The Honolulu Museum of Art, located in the heart of Hawaii's vibrant capital, stands as a premier cultural institution in the Pacific. Established in 1927 by Anna Rice Cooke, a patron of the arts and daughter of early missionaries, the museum was built on her belief that Hawaii could be a central point where the arts of the East and the West meet and influence each other. Today, it houses one of the most extensive collections of Asian and Pan-Pacific art in the United States, along with classical and contemporary collections from around the world.

The museum's collection features over 50,000 works, ranging from ancient times to the present. Key highlights include traditional Asian art, 19th- and 20th-century European and American paintings, and a dynamic array of contemporary art. The museum is particularly noted for its collection of Japanese woodblock prints, Chinese ceramics, African art, and works of such renowned artists as Van Gogh, Gauguin, and Picasso.

Architecturally, the Honolulu Museum of Art is a reflection of its cultural philosophy. The main building combines elements of traditional Hawaiian and Mediterranean styles, creating a serene and inviting atmosphere. The museum's layout encourages a natural flow from one exhibit to another, amidst courtyards and gardens that integrate tropical nature with the art on display, making it a peaceful oasis in the bustling city.

The museum is also committed to education and outreach, offering a wide range of public programs including film screenings in the Doris Duke Theatre, art classes, workshops, lectures, and guided tours that enhance the visitor experience and deepen understanding of the arts. The museum's Art School, located across the street, provides classes and workshops for children and adults, fostering local talent and supporting the arts community in Hawaii.

One of the most captivating aspects of the Honolulu Museum of Art is its engagement with the local community. It hosts annual events such as the "ARTafterDARK" series, which turns the museum into a lively venue for music, dancing, and art activities, drawing a diverse crowd of art lovers and newcomers alike.

30.   Ala Moana Center

Ala Moana Center, located in Honolulu, Hawaii, is the largest open-air shopping center in the world. Since its opening in 1959, Ala Moana has been a pivotal part of Hawaii's retail landscape, offering a unique shopping experience in the heart of the Pacific. It currently features over 350 stores on four levels, ranging from luxury brands to popular national chains, along with a variety of entertainment and dining options.

Spanning over 2.4 million square feet of retail space, Ala Moana Center is not only a shopper's paradise but also a major entertainment hub in Honolulu. The center is home to high-end boutiques such as Chanel, Louis Vuitton, and Prada, as well as department stores like Nordstrom and Neiman Marcus. It also includes a diverse array of specialty stores, offering everything from local Hawaiian apparel and crafts to the latest in tech gadgets.

In addition to its vast shopping offerings, Ala Moana Center is known for its Centerstage, one of the world's largest outdoor amphitheaters, which hosts over 500 performances a year ranging from hula dancing to holiday parades and live music. These performances highlight local culture and talent, making the shopping center a lively gathering place for both residents and tourists.

Dining at Ala Moana Center is a treat with options that cater to every taste and budget. The center boasts a wide range of culinary delights, from fast food to fine dining and everything in between. The Makai Market Food Court offers a variety of local and international cuisine, while restaurants such as Mariposa and Morton's The Steakhouse provide upscale dining experiences with views of the Pacific Ocean.

Moreover, Ala Moana's recent expansions have focused on creating a more visitor-friendly environment, featuring lush tropical landscaping, natural light, and open walkways that embrace Hawaii's natural beauty. The addition of the Ewa Wing has further enhanced the center's offerings, adding more luxury retailers and dining options.

For visitors, Ala Moana Center is more than just a shopping destination; it's a vibrant part of Honolulu's social fabric, offering a glimpse into the lifestyle of the Pacific.

Maui

1.   Haleakala National Park

Haleakala National Park, located on the island of Maui, is an expansive area that stretches across the island's eastern and southern coasts. The park is named after its crowning feature, Haleakala Crater, which is a massive shield volcano that forms more than 75% of the Maui landmass. Renowned for its breathtaking landscapes that range from stark volcanic terrains to lush tropical rainforests, this national park offers a unique glimpse into Hawaii's diverse natural beauty.

One of the park's most famous activities is watching the sunrise from the summit of Haleakala, standing at over 10,000 feet above sea level. Visitors often trek to the summit in the early hours of the morning to witness the spectacular dawn breaking over the crater, a spiritual experience for many that symbolize renewal and the immense beauty of nature. The view encompasses the entire island and parts of the neighboring islands on clear days.

Haleakala is also known for its astounding ecological diversity. The park is home to numerous endemic species, some of which are found nowhere else on the planet, such as the nene (Hawaiian goose), the state bird of Hawaii, and the silversword plant, which blooms spectacularly once in its life before dying. The park's varied elevations and climates support distinct ecosystems, from the barren moon-like landscape at the summit to the verdant coastal Kipahulu area, which features waterfalls and pools.

Hiking in Haleakala offers a variety of trails that cater to all fitness levels. Visitors can explore the Sliding Sands Trail that descends into the crater, offering stunning views of the volcanic landscape and its unique flora. In contrast, the Pipiwai Trail in the Kipahulu District leads hikers past giant banyan trees, a vast bamboo forest, and eventually to the impressive 400-foot Waimoku Falls.

2.   Wai'anapanapa State Park

Wai'anapanapa State Park, nestled along the road to Hana on Maui's northeast coast, encompasses 122 acres of volcanic coastline and offers some of the most unique and stunning landscapes in Hawaii. Known for its striking black sand beach, ancient lava tubes, native hala forests, and sacred Hawaiian sites, Wai'anapanapa provides a rich tapestry of natural and cultural history.

The park's standout feature is Pa'iloa Beach, with its jet-black sand formed from crushed lava rock. This dramatic beach is not only a great spot for photography but also offers excellent opportunities for tide pooling and sea cave exploration. The stark contrast of the deep blue ocean waves against the black sand and lush green foliage creates a breathtaking scene.

Beyond the beach, Wai'anapanapa boasts a network of hiking trails that offer panoramic views of the rugged coastline and lead to various historical and archaeological sites. One of the notable trails includes the ancient King's Highway, which visitors can follow to explore old religious temples (heiaus) and burial sites, providing insight into the area's significance in Hawaiian culture and history.

Another highlight is the blowhole that produces powerful sprays of seawater during high tide, creating a natural spectacle that draws spectators. Additionally, the park features freshwater caves that, according to legend, were the scene of a tragic event in Hawaiian folklore. These caves allow for a quiet moment to reflect on the lore and history of the land.

Wai'anapanapa State Park also offers picnicking facilities and camping areas, making it an ideal spot for longer visits to immerse oneself in nature's serenity and the area's cultural stories. Whether you come to witness the unique black sand beach, explore historical sites, or hike along the scenic trails, Wai'anapanapa State Park offers a profound connection to Maui's natural beauty and cultural heritage.

3.   Road to Hana

The Road to Hana is one of the most famous drives in the world, renowned not just for its final destination, but for the journey itself. Stretching over 64 miles from Kahului to the remote town of Hana on Maui's lush eastern coast, this drive is a must-experience for anyone visiting the island. The route is characterized by its narrow one-lane bridges, hairpin turns, and stunning views of cliffs, waterfalls, and the expansive Pacific Ocean.

The drive typically starts in Kahului, winding through rainforests and past cascading waterfalls, with plenty of stops that invite drivers to pause and soak in the scenery. Among the most popular stops are the Twin Falls, the Garden of Eden Arboretum, and the Waikamoi Ridge Trail. Each offers unique experiences from swimming in freshwater pools, exploring lush botanical gardens, to hiking through bamboo forests.

The town of Hana itself is a peaceful, rural community that feels worlds away from the busier tourist spots of Maui. Here, visitors can enjoy a slower pace of life and explore attractions such as the Hana Cultural Center & Museum, which provides insights into the area's history and culture, and Hana Bay, a picturesque beach perfect for relaxing after the long drive.

One of the highlights near Hana is the 'Ohe'o Gulch, also known as the Seven Sacred Pools, part of the Haleakala National Park. It's a beautifully scenic area where water flows through a series of lovely pools and waterfalls. Just beyond Hana is the Pi'ilanihale Heiau, one of the largest ancient Hawaiian temple platforms, which adds a significant cultural dimension to the visit.

The Road to Hana is more than just a scenic drive; it's an adventure that tests patience and rewards travelers with some of the most stunning vistas and experiences Maui has to offer. It encapsulates the island's spirit of adventure and natural beauty, making it an unforgettable journey for those who take it.

4. Makawao Town

Makawao Town, nestled on the rural northwest slopes of Haleakala on Maui, is a charming upcountry town that blends the island's paniolo (Hawaiian cowboy) heritage with its artsy present. Known for its rustic atmosphere and vibrant arts scene, Makawao is a delightful mix of old and new, where traditional Hawaiian culture intersects with modern influences.

Historically, Makawao has its roots in the paniolo culture of the late 19th and early 20th centuries when cattle ranching was a significant industry in Hawaii. Today, this heritage is celebrated in the town's architecture, museums, and the annual Makawao Rodeo, which attracts paniolo from all over the islands. Walking through the town, visitors can see remnants of its cowboy past in the storefronts designed with rustic charm and local businesses catering to both residents and tourists.

The town is also a hub for artists and artisans, making it a significant part of Maui's art scene. Numerous galleries and workshops line the streets, showcasing everything from traditional Hawaiian crafts to contemporary art. Local artists often open their studios to visitors, offering a unique opportunity to watch them at work and to purchase original pieces.

Makawao is also known for its eclectic shopping and dining options. Boutiques featuring handcrafted jewelry, clothing, and home decor items are popular stops for those looking for unique finds. The culinary scene is equally diverse, with cafes and restaurants offering a blend of local cuisine and international dishes, often prepared with locally sourced ingredients.

The town's laid-back atmosphere, combined with its cultural richness and artistic vitality, makes Makawao Town a captivating destination for those looking to experience a different side of Maui away from the typical beach-focused tourist paths. Whether you're interested in the history of Hawaiian cowboys, looking to immerse yourself in the local art scene, or simply seeking a peaceful retreat in the cool upcountry climate, Makawao offers a warm and welcoming experience.

5.   Ho'okipa Beach Park

Ho'okipa Beach Park, located on Maui's north shore near the historic town of Paia, is internationally renowned as one of the premier windsurfing spots in the world. This picturesque park is not only a hotspot for windsurfing but also serves as a prime location for surfing, kiteboarding, and stand-up paddleboarding, attracting both amateur enthusiasts and professional athletes alike.

The name Ho'okipa means "hospitality" in Hawaiian, and the beach truly lives up to its name by welcoming visitors with its spectacular ocean views and excellent recreational opportunities. The beach features impressive waves and consistent trade winds that create ideal conditions for windsurfing nearly year-round. The winter months often bring larger swells that make for exciting surfing and windsurfing competitions, which are held frequently at Ho'okipa.

Aside from water sports, Ho'okipa Beach Park is also famous for its sea turtle population. Every evening, Hawaiian green sea turtles climb onto the beach to rest, providing a unique wildlife viewing opportunity for visitors. The beach park includes an overlook area that allows people to observe these magnificent creatures while maintaining a respectful distance, ensuring the turtles are not disturbed.

The park's facilities include picnic areas, restrooms, showers, and ample parking, making it an ideal spot for a day trip. Visitors can relax on the beach, enjoy a picnic with family and friends, or simply watch the thrilling action on the water from the beach's sandy shores or the grassy hillside above.

Ho'okipa Beach Park also serves as an excellent photographic venue, especially during sunset when the sky and sea are lit with vibrant colors, providing a stunning backdrop against the silhouettes of windsurfers and the natural scenery.

For those who love the ocean, are fascinated by marine wildlife, or simply enjoy watching world-class water sports, Ho'okipa Beach Park offers a dynamic and inviting environment where all these interests converge, making it a must-visit destination on Maui's beautiful north shore.

6.   Paia Town

Paia Town, nestled on the north coast of Maui, is a quaint and colorful town that serves as the gateway to the famous Road to Hana. Known for its laid-back hippie vibe and plantation-era architecture, Paia is a charming blend of history, culture, and modern eclecticism, making it a compelling stop for travelers exploring Maui.

This small, bustling town was once a thriving sugar cane plantation town but has since transformed into a vibrant community with a strong emphasis on arts, local cuisine, and unique shopping experiences. Paia is home to a diverse array of boutiques, surf shops, art galleries, and restaurants that cater to all tastes and preferences, from organic vegetarian cafes to local seafood eateries.

One of the highlights of Paia Town is its strong commitment to local arts and culture. Numerous galleries and studios showcase the work of local artists, ranging from traditional Hawaiian crafts to contemporary art. The town also hosts frequent cultural events and music nights, which contribute to its lively atmosphere and allow visitors to experience the local community spirit.

Paia's location also makes it a perfect base for those looking to explore the natural beauties of Maui's north shore, including nearby beaches like Baldwin Beach Park and Ho'okipa Beach Park, known for excellent swimming, windsurfing, and sunbathing. The town's proximity to these beaches, combined with its bohemian charm, makes it a popular destination for those seeking a less commercialized experience of Maui.

For travelers looking for a place with rustic charm, eclectic shopping, and a warm, welcoming atmosphere, Paia Town offers a delightful experience that combines the allure of old Hawaii with the vibrancy of contemporary island culture.

7.   Iao Valley State Park

Iao Valley State Park, nestled in the heart of Maui's central mountains, is a lush, 4,000-acre valley rich in natural beauty and cultural significance. Known for its historical importance as the site of the Battle of Kepaniwai where King Kamehameha I clashed with Maui's army in his quest to unite the Hawaiian Islands, the park offers a serene escape into nature and a chance to delve into Hawaiian history.

The park's most iconic feature is the Iao Needle, a 1,200-foot tall green-mantled rock outcropping that stands as a natural monument amidst the valley. This striking pinnacle is best viewed from the park's well-maintained walkways and viewing platform, which provide spectacular sights of the needle and the surrounding lush valley walls draped in tropical foliage.

The Iao Valley is characterized by its deep ridges and mist-covered peaks, formed by erosion of the softer rock by the Iao Stream and other natural elements. This lush area receives ample rainfall, supporting a vibrant green landscape that offers a stark contrast to Maui's coastal areas. The park is home to various native plants and birds, many of which are unique to Hawaii, making it a great spot for nature lovers and bird watchers.

Aside from its natural beauty, Iao Valley State Park is imbued with a sense of tranquility and spiritual significance. The valley was considered a sacred site by the native Hawaiians, and many historical artifacts and remnants have been found here. Several walking trails allow visitors to explore the area further, including paths that lead to the stream, where you can often see traditional Hawaiian taro fields in cultivation.

Visitors to Iao Valley State Park can also learn about the ecological efforts and cultural preservation activities taking place in the valley, which aim to maintain the area's natural environment and respect its historical heritage. Whether you're interested in hiking, photography, or simply enjoying a peaceful retreat in one of Maui's most beautiful landscapes, Iao Valley State Park offers an enriching and memorable experience.

8.   Kapalua Bay Beach

Kapalua Bay Beach, located on the northwest coast of Maui, is frequently ranked among the best beaches in the United States. Known for its golden sand, crystal clear waters, and natural protection by two lava promontories, which provide a sheltered sanctuary perfect for swimming and snorkeling, Kapalua Bay offers visitors a quintessential Hawaiian beach experience.

The bay's calm waters make it an ideal spot for snorkelers of all levels. The coral reefs are home to a vibrant array of marine life, including colorful fish, sea turtles, and occasionally, spinner dolphins. Snorkeling near the rocks on either side of the bay provides the best opportunities to observe the underwater biodiversity that Kapalua Bay is celebrated for.

Kapalua Bay Beach is also popular for its scenic beauty and recreational opportunities. The beach is lined with palm trees offering ample shade for picnics or relaxing with a good book. For those looking to be more active, there are walking trails along the coastline that offer beautiful views of the ocean and nearby islands.

The beach's proximity to the Kapalua Resort means that visitors have easy access to a range of amenities, including upscale restaurants, golf courses, and tennis courts. The resort also hosts the annual Kapalua Wine and Food Festival, which attracts gourmets and connoisseurs from around the world, adding an extra layer of allure to visiting Kapalua Bay.

With its stunning natural setting, abundant marine life, and luxurious amenities, Kapalua Bay Beach not only offers a relaxing beach day but also a touch of sophistication to your Hawaiian vacation, making it a must-visit for anyone traveling to Maui. Whether you are snorkeling in its clear waters, sunbathing on its soft sands, or enjoying the amenities of the nearby resort, Kapalua Bay Beach promises a delightful and fulfilling experience.

9. Kaanapali Beach

Kaanapali Beach, located on the west coast of Maui, is one of Hawaii's most iconic and beloved beaches. Stretching over three miles of golden sand against the backdrop of crystal-clear waters and luxurious resorts, this beach was once a retreat for the royalty of Maui and now serves as a prime destination for visitors from around the world.

Kaanapali Beach is renowned for its breathtaking beauty and wide range of activities suitable for all ages. The beach is most famous for its cliff diving ceremony off the northernmost cliff called Puu Kekaa, or Black Rock. Each evening at sunset, a cliff diver lights the torches along the cliff and then dives into the water, a reenactment of a feat by Maui's revered King Kahekili. This tradition adds a cultural touch to the stunning natural scenery of Kaanapali Beach.

For water enthusiasts, the beach offers excellent conditions for swimming, snorkeling, and paddleboarding. The clear waters around Black Rock are known for some of the best snorkeling in Maui, with vibrant coral reefs that are home to a variety of tropical fish and sea turtles. Additionally, parasailing, jet skiing, and surfing are popular activities that visitors can enjoy here.

Along the beachfront, the Kaanapali Beachwalk is a scenic pathway that connects the luxury resorts and condos, offering easy access to the many shops, restaurants, and bars that line the beach. Visitors can explore high-end boutiques, dine at oceanfront restaurants, or enjoy a cocktail while watching the sun dip below the horizon.

Kaanapali Beach also hosts several world-class golf courses, providing stunning ocean views for golfers. The combination of challenging play and the serene beach environment makes for an unforgettable golfing experience.

With its stunning natural beauty, rich cultural activities, and luxurious amenities, Kaanapali Beach epitomizes the ideal tropical getaway, making it a must-visit destination for anyone traveling to Maui.

10.   Lahaina Historic Town

Lahaina Historic Town, once the capital of the Hawaiian Kingdom and a busy whaling port, is now one of Maui's most vibrant cultural hotspots. This coastal town is steeped in history, with its well-preserved 19th-century architecture and a lively atmosphere that draws visitors looking to experience a blend of Hawaiian culture, history, and modern day entertainment.

Walking through Front Street, the town's main thoroughfare, visitors can explore a variety of shops, art galleries, and restaurants. Lahaina's rich history is showcased in several landmarks such as the Lahaina Historic Trail, which includes 62 historic sites like the old Lahaina Lighthouse, the U.S. Seamen's Hospital, and the Pioneer Inn, one of Hawaii's oldest hotels.

One of Lahaina's most famous landmarks is the Banyan Tree Park, where a massive banyan tree planted in 1873 spans nearly an acre with its complex root system. The tree provides shade for artisans and performers, creating a lively gathering place for visitors and locals alike.

Lahaina is also known for its significant cultural events, such as the annual Halloween celebration, which transforms Front Street into a festive party with costumes, live music, and food. Additionally, the town hosts the Lahaina Restoration Foundation's free monthly Hawaiian Music Series, further enhancing its cultural appeal.

Lahaina's connection to the ocean is ever-present. The town's harbor offers boat trips for whale watching, fishing, and snorkeling, allowing visitors to experience the marine beauty that surrounds Maui. Lahaina's importance in the whaling industry is chronicled in the Whalers Village Museum, which offers insights into its maritime history.

Today, Lahaina is not just a relic of the past but a lively center of Hawaiian culture and nightlife, making it an essential visit for anyone wanting to experience the heart and soul of Maui.

11.   Banyan Tree Fine Art Gallery

The Banyan Tree Fine Art Gallery, located in Lahaina, Maui, is a renowned art destination that showcases a diverse range of artwork by local and international artists. Situated under the iconic Banyan Tree, from which it takes its name, the gallery is a cultural landmark within the historic town, offering visitors a chance to explore Hawaii's vibrant art scene in a unique and inspiring setting.

This gallery specializes in fine art, including paintings, sculptures, and mixed media pieces that reflect the rich cultural heritage and natural beauty of Hawaii. The artworks often depict Hawaiian landscapes, seascapes, flora, and fauna, as well as cultural motifs that convey the spirit of the islands. The gallery's commitment to promoting both established and emerging artists makes it a dynamic place where art lovers can discover new talents and appreciate well-known masters.

Visitors to the Banyan Tree Fine Art Gallery are treated to a visual feast that includes traditional Hawaiian art forms as well as contemporary interpretations that push creative boundaries. The gallery also hosts exhibitions and events that engage the community and tourists alike, such as artist workshops, live painting demonstrations, and cultural presentations that enhance the understanding of the art on display.

In addition to showcasing art, the gallery is a place of interaction and learning, where visitors can meet artists and discuss their works, gaining deeper insights into their creative processes and the inspirations behind their pieces. This direct engagement with artists adds a personal touch to the gallery experience, making it more memorable and enriching.

The Banyan Tree Fine Art Gallery not only enhances Lahaina's reputation as a cultural hub but also serves as a bridge connecting the local community with the global art scene. It is an essential destination for anyone interested in the arts and looking to explore the diverse expressions of creativity found on Maui.

12.   Olowalu Petroglyphs

The Olowalu Petroglyphs, also known as Pu'u Kilea, are ancient rock carvings located in the Olowalu Valley on the island of Maui. This significant cultural site provides a fascinating glimpse into the lives and beliefs of the early Hawaiians. The petroglyphs are etched into large basalt boulders and cliffs, featuring over 100 distinct carvings that date back several centuries.

The carvings at Olowalu include a variety of designs and motifs, such as human figures, animals, and geometric patterns. These images are believed to represent aspects of daily life, spiritual beliefs, and important events in the community, such as births and victories in battle. Some carvings are thought to be depictions of Hawaiian gods and ancestral spirits, reflecting the spiritual practices and worldview of the Native Hawaiian people.

Visiting the Olowalu Petroglyphs involves a short hike into the valley, where the petroglyphs can be viewed from a designated platform to protect the site from damage. The walk through the Olowalu area also offers beautiful views of the surrounding landscape, characterized by lush vegetation and the backdrop of the West Maui Mountains.

The site is not only a valuable archaeological resource but also a sacred place for the Hawaiian people. Efforts have been made to preserve the petroglyphs and ensure that they are respected by visitors. Interpretive signs provide information about the history and significance of the carvings, helping to educate the public about this important cultural heritage.

The Olowalu Petroglyphs offer a direct link to Hawaii's past, making them a must-visit for history enthusiasts and anyone interested in the rich cultural tapestry of the islands. They serve as a reminder of the deep connection between the Hawaiian people and their land, and the enduring legacy of their ancient traditions.

Together, these destinations offer a deep dive into the cultural and historical richness of Maui, providing visitors with a broad perspective on the island's artistic contributions and its preserved ancient sites. Each location offers a unique experience, from the artistic expressions at the Banyan Tree Fine Art Gallery to the ancient narratives captured in the Olowalu Petroglyphs.

13.   Maui Ocean Center

The Maui Ocean Center, located in Maʻalaea Harbor, is a state-of-the-art aquarium and oceanography institute that provides visitors with a closer look at Hawaii's unique marine environment. Opened in 1998, the center is committed to fostering understanding, wonder, and respect for Hawaii's marine life. Featuring a collection of Hawaiian reefs, fish, and marine species, the center offers an immersive experience into the underwater world surrounding the islands.

Spanning three acres, the Maui Ocean Center houses over 60 interactive exhibits, including touch pools, a turtle lagoon, and a two-story shark tank. One of the most striking features is the 750,000-gallon Open Ocean exhibit, which includes a 54-foot long, 240-degree acrylic tunnel that allows visitors to walk through as sharks, rays, and hundreds of fish swim around them. This exhibit provides an unparalleled view of marine life and is a highlight for all visitors.

In addition to its displays, the Maui Ocean Center places a strong emphasis on education and conservation. The center offers daily presentations by marine biologists and naturalists who provide insights into the behavior and habitats of marine creatures, as well as the challenges they face, such as climate change and pollution. These educational programs are designed to inspire visitors to appreciate and conserve the delicate marine ecosystems.

The Maui Ocean Center also participates in reef restoration projects and endangered species protection, actively contributing to the preservation of Hawaii's natural heritage. For example, the center runs a coral propagation program, which helps to regenerate damaged reefs around Maui.

Visitors to the Maui Ocean Center can also enjoy the Seascape Restaurant, which offers ocean-view dining, and the Maui Ocean Treasures gift shop, which features a wide array of marine-themed souvenirs, from jewelry to educational books. Both facilities enhance the visitor experience by combining leisure with learning and shopping with environmental awareness.

14.   Humpback Whale National Marine Sanctuary

The Humpback Whale National Marine Sanctuary, located in the waters off Maui, was established in 1992 to protect humpback whales and their habitat in Hawaii. The sanctuary, which spans over 1,400 square miles, is one of the world's most important breeding, calving, and nursing grounds for the North Pacific humpback whales, who migrate from the cold waters of Alaska to the warm Hawaiian seas each winter.

From December to April, visitors to the sanctuary can witness these magnificent creatures in their natural environment. The sanctuary provides an invaluable opportunity to observe humpback whales as they engage in courtship, birthing, and rearing their calves. Whale watching tours, guided by knowledgeable naturalists, offer insights into the behavior and characteristics of these whales, enhancing public understanding and appreciation of one of the ocean's largest mammals.

The sanctuary also conducts and supports scientific research aimed at better understanding the humpback whales and the threats they face from human activities and environmental changes. This research is critical for developing effective management and conservation strategies to protect the whales and their habitat.

Educational programs are a key component of the sanctuary's mission. The sanctuary operates the Hawaiian Islands Humpback Whale National Marine Sanctuary Visitor Center on Maui, where visitors can learn about the whales through interactive displays, educational talks, and documentary films. The center also hosts community events and school programs to engage the public in conservation efforts and to spread awareness about marine protection.

The Humpback Whale National Marine Sanctuary not only offers a rare glimpse into the lives of one of the most awe-inspiring marine species but also plays a critical role in the global effort to protect them. Witnessing humpback whales in their natural setting can be a transformative experience, emphasizing the beauty of marine life and the importance of ocean conservation.

15.   Wailea Beach

Wailea Beach, situated on the south shore of Maui, is one of the island's most exquisite beaches, renowned for its golden sands, crystal-clear waters, and luxurious surroundings. Flanked by high-end resorts and manicured pathways, Wailea Beach offers both a taste of luxury and the natural beauty of Hawaii's coastline.

The beach itself is relatively wide with soft, golden sand and provides ample space for sunbathing, building sandcastles, or enjoying a leisurely stroll along the shore. The waters at Wailea Beach are generally calm, thanks to the protective offshore reefs, making it an excellent spot for swimming and snorkeling. Visitors often remark on the clarity of the water and the abundance of marine life, including colorful fish and occasionally sea turtles, which can be spotted near the rocky points on either side of the beach.

Wailea Beach is well-equipped with amenities, including showers, restrooms, and public loungers. Lifeguards are on duty to ensure the safety of all beachgoers, making it a secure choice for families with children. Moreover, the beach's proximity to several luxury resorts means that visitors have easy access to upscale dining options, spa services, and other resort amenities, even if they are not staying at the resorts.

Beyond water activities, Wailea Beach is popular for its stunning sunsets. Many visitors gather in the evenings to watch as the sun dips below the horizon, painting the sky in shades of orange, pink, and purple. This daily spectacle adds to the romantic and tranquil atmosphere of the beach, making it a favorite spot for couples and those seeking a peaceful retreat.

In addition to its natural and recreational offerings, Wailea Beach hosts several annual events, including a renowned film festival that brings together filmmakers and cinephiles from around the world. These events add a cultural dimension to the beach, making it not just a place for relaxation and enjoyment but also a hub of cultural activity.

Wailea Beach embodies the luxury and beauty of Maui's coast and is a must-visit destination for anyone looking to experience the best of what the Hawaiian Islands have to offer.

16.   MauiWine

Nestled in the rolling hills of Ulupalakua Ranch on the slopes of Haleakala, MauiWine is Hawaii's premier winery, offering a unique viticultural experience that blends rich Hawaiian history with the art of winemaking. Established in 1974, MauiWine has grown from a small experimental vineyard into a renowned winery, attracting visitors from around the world eager to taste its unique wines and explore its historic grounds.

MauiWine is known for its distinctive wines, which include traditional grape wines as well as tropical fruit wines made from pineapple and passion fruit. The winery takes pride in incorporating local ingredients and using innovative techniques that reflect the island's climate and agricultural heritage. One of its most celebrated offerings is the Pineapple Sparkling Wine, a refreshing and exotic drink that captures the essence of tropical Hawaii.

Visitors to MauiWine can participate in guided tasting tours that provide an in-depth look at the winemaking process and offer samples of various wines. The tasting room, located in the historic King's Cottage, allows guests to savor the flavors of the wines while learning about the history of the winery and the region. The cottage itself dates back to the 1870s when it served as a guesthouse for King Kalakaua, the last king of Hawaii.

The estate also features beautiful, expansive grounds that guests are encouraged to explore. These include the Old Jail, built in the 1850s and once used as a temporary holding area for rowdy cowboys from the ranch, and the lush gardens that surround the winery, offering panoramic views of the vineyards and the valley below.

In addition to wine tastings and tours, MauiWine hosts special events throughout the year, including harvest festivals, food and wine pairings, and live music performances, making it a vibrant part of Maui's cultural scene.

MauiWine offers a delightful experience for wine lovers and those interested in the unique agricultural practices of Hawaii. It stands as a testament to the diversity and richness of Maui's agricultural and cultural landscapes, offering a taste of local tradition and modern innovation in every glass.

17. Makena Beach State Park (Big Beach)

Makena Beach State Park, affectionately known as Big Beach, is a stunning stretch of golden sand nestled along the southwest coast of Maui, Hawaii. Renowned for its vast expanse and picturesque setting, Big Beach is a favorite among locals and visitors alike, drawing beach enthusiasts seeking sun, surf, and natural beauty.

While Big Beach's expansive sands are perfect for sunbathing and picnicking, the waters off its coast are known for their powerful shore break and strong currents. As such, swimming at Big Beach can be challenging, especially for inexperienced swimmers or young children. However, for more adventurous visitors, the waves offer opportunities for bodyboarding and bodysurfing, providing an exhilarating aquatic experience.

For those seeking calmer waters, adjacent to Big Beach lies Little Beach, a smaller, more sheltered cove known for its tranquil turquoise waters and clothing-optional atmosphere. Accessible via a short hike over the rocky outcrop at the north end of Big Beach, Little Beach offers a secluded retreat for sunbathers and swimmers looking for a more intimate beach experience.

Beyond its natural beauty, Makena Beach State Park is also home to a variety of recreational activities and amenities. Picnic tables and grills are available for beachside barbecues, while showers and restrooms provide convenience for visitors. Lifeguards are stationed at the beach during peak hours, ensuring the safety of swimmers and beachgoers.

In addition to its recreational offerings, Makena Beach State Park boasts stunning panoramic views of the surrounding coastline and neighboring islands, including the iconic silhouette of Molokini Crater to the northeast. Visitors can admire the scenic vistas from the beach or venture to nearby vantage points, such as Pu'u Olai, a dormant volcanic cinder cone that offers sweeping views of the coastline and the Pacific Ocean.

18.   Molokini Crater

Molokini Crater is a unique and mesmerizing geological formation located off the coast of Maui, Hawaii. Situated between the islands of Maui and Kahoʻolawe, this crescent-shaped volcanic crater rises from the depths of the Pacific Ocean, creating a stunning underwater sanctuary for marine life and a renowned snorkeling and diving destination.

Formed over thousands of years through volcanic activity, Molokini Crater is renowned for its pristine waters and exceptional visibility, with underwater visibility often exceeding 100 feet. This clarity offers unparalleled opportunities for underwater exploration, allowing visitors to marvel at the vibrant coral reefs, colorful tropical fish, and diverse marine species that inhabit the crater's submerged slopes.

Molokini's unique crescent shape creates a natural protective barrier from ocean swells and currents, resulting in calm, sheltered waters within its submerged caldera. This tranquil environment makes Molokini an ideal habitat for a wide array of marine life, including reef fish, sea turtles, moray eels, and octopuses, as well as larger pelagic species such as sharks and rays.

For snorkelers and divers, Molokini Crater offers a captivating underwater playground teeming with life. Guided snorkeling and diving tours provide access to the crater's most pristine reef areas, where visitors can swim among colorful coral gardens and encounter an abundance of tropical fish darting in and out of the coral formations.

In addition to its vibrant marine ecosystem, Molokini Crater holds cultural and ecological significance for the Hawaiian people. Known as a puʻu kāne (sacred place) in Hawaiian culture, the crater is revered as a spiritual site and is steeped in legends and lore passed down through generations.

Access to Molokini Crater is restricted to authorized tour operators and private vessels, ensuring the protection and preservation of this fragile marine environment. Visitors can embark on snorkeling and diving excursions departing from nearby harbors on Maui, with experienced guides providing educational insights into the crater's ecology and history.

Hawaii (The Big Island)

1.   Ka Lae (South Point)

Ka Lae, also known as South Point, is a mesmerizing destination located at the southernmost tip of Hawaii, specifically the Big Island. This remote and rugged area is not only geographically significant as the southernmost point of the United States but also holds great cultural and natural importance.

Standing at Ka Lae, visitors are greeted with breathtaking views of the vast Pacific Ocean stretching out as far as the eye can see. The rugged cliffs and coastline, sculpted by the relentless forces of wind and waves, create a dramatic and awe-inspiring landscape. The sound of the crashing waves against the rocky shoreline adds to the sense of wild beauty that permeates the area.

Aside from its natural splendor, Ka Lae holds deep cultural significance for the Native Hawaiian people. It is believed to be the site of the first Polynesian landfall in Hawaii, marking the arrival of the ancient Polynesian voyagers who navigated the vast ocean using only the stars and ocean currents. As such, Ka Lae is revered as a sacred site and a place of great spiritual importance.

One of the notable features of Ka Lae is its historic fishing village, where traditional Hawaiian fishing practices have been passed down through generations. Visitors can observe locals casting their lines into the ocean from the rocky shoreline, using traditional methods to catch fish and other marine life. The fishing village offers a fascinating glimpse into Hawaii's rich maritime heritage and the enduring connection between the Hawaiian people and the sea.

For the adventurous traveler, Ka Lae offers opportunities for cliff diving into the crystal-clear waters below. Brave souls can leap from the towering cliffs into the ocean, experiencing an adrenaline rush and a unique perspective of the rugged coastline.

2. Green Sand Beach at Papakolea

The Green Sand Beach at Papakolea is a remarkable natural wonder nestled along the southern coast of the Big Island of Hawaii. Renowned for its unique olive-green sand and stunning coastal scenery, this secluded beach offers visitors an unforgettable and otherworldly experience.

Accessible via a scenic hike or a rugged 4x4 drive, the Green Sand Beach is a hidden gem tucked away from the hustle and bustle of tourist crowds. As visitors approach the beach, they are greeted by the sight of the vibrant green sand, a result of the presence of the mineral olivine in the volcanic rocks surrounding the area. The contrast between the lush green cliffs, the turquoise waters of the Pacific Ocean, and the striking green sand creates a surreal and captivating scene.

Once at the beach, visitors can relax on the soft sands, soak up the sun, and take in the breathtaking coastal views. The tranquil atmosphere and remote location make it an ideal spot for picnicking, sunbathing, and beachcombing. Adventurous travelers can also explore the rocky shoreline and tide pools, where they may encounter colorful marine life and unique volcanic formations.

While swimming at the Green Sand Beach is possible, caution is advised due to strong currents and powerful waves. It's essential to exercise caution and adhere to any posted safety warnings to ensure a safe and enjoyable experience.

In addition to its natural beauty, the Green Sand Beach holds cultural significance for the Native Hawaiian people. It is considered a sacred site, and visitors are encouraged to treat it with respect and reverence. As such, it's essential to practice responsible tourism and leave only footprints behind.

Overall, the Green Sand Beach at Papakolea offers a truly unique and unforgettable experience for those willing to venture off the beaten path. From its stunning green sands to its pristine coastal scenery, this hidden gem showcases the raw beauty and natural wonders of Hawaii's Big Island in all its glory.

3.   Punaluu Bake Shop

Located on the southeastern coast of the Big Island of Hawaii, Punaluu Bake Shop is a charming and historic establishment famous for its delicious Hawaiian sweetbreads and pastries. Founded in 1991, the bake shop has become a beloved landmark and a must-visit destination for both locals and tourists exploring the island.

As visitors approach the bake shop, they are greeted by the irresistible aroma of freshly baked goods wafting through the air. The quaint and colorful building, adorned with tropical flowers and Hawaiian decor, exudes a warm and inviting atmosphere, inviting guests to step inside and indulge their senses.

One of the highlights of Punaluu Bake Shop is its mouthwatering assortment of Hawaiian sweetbreads, including traditional flavors such as taro, coconut, and guava, as well as unique creations like lilikoi (passion fruit) and pineapple. These sweetbreads are baked fresh daily using time-honored recipes passed down through generations, ensuring a taste of authentic Hawaiian flavor with every bite.

In addition to its signature sweetbreads, the bake shop offers a tempting selection of pastries, cakes, and cookies, all made with locally sourced ingredients and a touch of aloha. Visitors can indulge in treats like buttery shortbread cookies, creamy coconut macadamia nut tarts, and decadent chocolate haupia (coconut pudding) pie, each crafted with care and attention to detail.

Beyond its delectable baked goods, Punaluu Bake Shop also offers a variety of Hawaiian-themed gifts and souvenirs, including t-shirts, mugs, and local artisan products. Guests can browse the shop's shelves for unique keepsakes and mementos to commemorate their visit to this beloved island institution.

While at Punaluu Bake Shop, visitors can also take advantage of the scenic picnic area located on the property. Surrounded by lush tropical foliage and fragrant flowers, this tranquil outdoor space provides the perfect setting for enjoying a leisurely meal or snack while soaking up the island's natural beauty.

4.   Black Sand Beach at Punalu'u

The Black Sand Beach at Punalu'u is a striking and picturesque destination located on the southeastern coast of the Big Island of Hawaii. Renowned for its unique black sand, rugged coastline, and serene ambiance, this iconic beach offers visitors a one-of-a-kind natural experience.

As visitors approach the beach, they are greeted by the sight of the dark volcanic sands stretching along the shoreline, contrasting starkly with the turquoise waters of the Pacific Ocean. The black sand is composed of finely ground lava rock, created by the volcanic activity that shaped the island millions of years ago. This geological phenomenon creates a dramatic and mesmerizing scene that captivates visitors from around the world.

The Black Sand Beach at Punalu'u is not only visually stunning but also serves as an important habitat for native wildlife, including endangered green sea turtles (honu). These majestic creatures can often be spotted basking on the warm sands or swimming in the crystal-clear waters just offshore. Visitors are reminded to maintain a respectful distance from the turtles and refrain from touching or disturbing them to ensure their safety and well-being.

In addition to its resident sea turtles, the beach offers excellent opportunities for swimming, snorkeling, and beachcombing. The calm and shallow waters are ideal for wading and exploring the colorful marine life that inhabits the nearby coral reefs. Snorkelers may encounter vibrant fish, graceful sea turtles, and other fascinating creatures that call the reef home.

The Black Sand Beach at Punalu'u is also steeped in cultural significance for the Native Hawaiian people. It is considered a sacred site and a place of great spiritual importance, with legends and stories passed down through generations about its origins and significance. Visitors are encouraged to treat the beach with respect and reverence, honoring its cultural heritage and natural beauty.

5.   Hawaii Volcanoes National Park

Hawaii Volcanoes National Park, located on the Big Island of Hawaii, is a mesmerizing destination that offers a unique glimpse into the powerful forces that shape our planet. Established in 1916, the park spans over 335,259 acres and encompasses two of the world's most active volcanoes: Kīlauea and Mauna Loa. This extraordinary landscape of volcanic craters, steam vents, and lava fields is a testament to the ever-changing nature of Earth.

One of the park's most remarkable features is Kīlauea, which has been erupting continuously since 1983. Visitors can witness the dramatic sight of molten lava flowing into the ocean, creating billowing steam clouds and expanding the island's coastline. The Crater Rim Drive, an 11-mile loop road, provides access to several overlooks and hiking trails, offering breathtaking views of the Kīlauea Caldera and the Halema'uma'u Crater, home to Pele, the Hawaiian goddess of fire and volcanoes.

Mauna Loa, the largest shield volcano on Earth, dominates the park's landscape. Though it is currently dormant, Mauna Loa has erupted 33 times since its first well-documented eruption in 1843. Adventurous visitors can hike to its summit, a challenging trek that rewards with stunning vistas of the island and the opportunity to stand on the world's largest volcano.

The park is not just about volcanoes; it also boasts lush rainforests, unique ecosystems, and an array of native Hawaiian plants and animals. The Kīlauea Iki Trail, a popular hiking route, takes visitors through a verdant rainforest before descending into a crater that was filled with lava during a 1959 eruption. The Thurston Lava Tube, another must-see, allows visitors to walk through a massive underground tunnel formed by flowing lava.

Hawaii Volcanoes National Park is also rich in cultural heritage. The Jaggar Museum and the Kīlauea Visitor Center offer exhibits on the geology, ecology, and cultural significance of the area. Ranger-led programs and guided tours provide deeper insights into the park's natural and cultural history. The park's landscapes are deeply intertwined with Hawaiian mythology and traditions, making it a place of profound spiritual significance.

6.   Lava Tree State Monument

Lava Tree State Monument, located in the Puna District of the Big Island of Hawaii, is a captivating site that showcases the remarkable interactions between lava flows and the natural environment. This 17-acre park is home to an extraordinary collection of lava trees, formed during a volcanic eruption in the late 18th century. These unique geological formations provide a fascinating glimpse into the island's volcanic history.

The lava trees at the monument were created when a fast-moving lava flow swept through a forested area, coating the trees in molten rock. As the lava cooled and solidified, it preserved the shape of the trees in stone, leaving behind hollow, cylindrical molds where the trees once stood. These eerie, yet beautiful, structures are a testament to the power of volcanic forces and the ability of nature to adapt and transform.

A loop trail, approximately one mile long, winds through the park, offering visitors an easy and enjoyable way to explore the lava trees and the surrounding landscape. Interpretive signs along the trail provide information about the formation of the lava trees, the types of vegetation in the area, and the volcanic activity that shaped the region. The trail is well-maintained and suitable for visitors of all ages and fitness levels, making it a great destination for families and casual hikers.

In addition to the lava trees, the park is home to a variety of native Hawaiian plants and bird species. The lush, tropical vegetation contrasts sharply with the stark, black lava formations, creating a striking and beautiful environment. The park's diverse flora includes ferns, orchids, and various types of native trees, providing ample opportunities for nature photography and bird watching.

Lava Tree State Monument also holds cultural significance for the Hawaiian people. The park is situated in an area that was historically inhabited by native Hawaiians, and the lava trees are considered to be a symbol of resilience and renewal. The monument serves as a reminder of the island's volcanic past and the ways in which the Hawaiian people have adapted to and revered their dynamic environment.

The Lyman Museum and Mission House, located in Hilo on the Big Island of Hawaii, offers a fascinating glimpse into the natural and cultural history of Hawaii. Established in 1931, the museum is named after David and Sarah Lyman, New England missionaries who arrived in Hawaii in the early 19th century. The museum complex consists of the historic Lyman Mission House, built in 1839, and a modern museum building that houses extensive collections of artifacts and exhibits.

The Lyman Mission House is the oldest wood-framed building on the Big Island and one of the oldest standing structures in Hawaii. It has been meticulously restored to its original condition, providing visitors with an authentic look at the daily lives of the missionaries and early settlers. Guided tours of the Mission House offer insights into the challenges and achievements of the Lyman family and their contributions to the development of Hilo and the surrounding areas.

Adjacent to the Mission House, the Lyman Museum features a diverse array of exhibits that cover a wide range of topics, from Hawaiian culture and history to the island's unique geology and natural history. The Earth Heritage Gallery showcases the volcanic origins of the Hawaiian Islands, with displays of lava rocks, minerals, and a stunning collection of Hawaiian gemstones. Interactive exhibits explain the geological processes that have shaped the islands and continue to influence their landscapes.

The Island Heritage Gallery delves into the rich cultural history of Hawaii, highlighting the traditions, beliefs, and lifestyles of the native Hawaiian people. The gallery features an impressive collection of artifacts, including ancient tools, weapons, and ceremonial objects. It also explores the impact of European and American contact on Hawaiian society, documenting the changes brought about by missionaries, traders, and settlers.

One of the museum's most popular exhibits is the John Howard Pierce Collection of Hawaiian Art, which includes a variety of traditional Hawaiian artifacts such as kapa (bark cloth), feather work, and lei (garlands). The collection provides a vivid representation of the artistry and craftsmanship of the Hawaiian people, showcasing their deep connection to nature and their cultural heritage.

8.   Rainbow Falls

Rainbow Falls, located in Hilo on the Big Island of Hawaii, is one of the island's most iconic and accessible natural attractions. Known in Hawaiian as Waianuenue, which means "rainbow water," this stunning waterfall lives up to its name with its ability to produce rainbows in the mist on sunny mornings. The falls are part of the Wailuku River, the longest river in Hawaii, and are easily accessible from downtown Hilo, making them a popular destination for both locals and tourists.

The waterfall cascades 80 feet over a lava cave into a large, serene pool surrounded by lush tropical vegetation. The cave behind the waterfall is said to be the home of Hina, an ancient Hawaiian goddess and the mother of the demigod Maui. According to Hawaiian mythology, Hina lived in the cave to escape from her son Maui's pranks and mischief. This legend adds a layer of cultural significance to the natural beauty of the site.

Visitors to Rainbow Falls can enjoy the spectacular view from a viewing platform located just a short walk from the parking area. The platform offers a clear, unobstructed view of the falls and the surrounding scenery, making it a perfect spot for photography and nature observation. Early morning is the best time to visit, as the angle of the sunlight creates beautiful rainbows in the mist, enhancing the magical atmosphere of the location.

In addition to the main viewing area, there are several short trails that allow visitors to explore the area around the falls. A set of stone steps leads to the top of the falls, where visitors can get a different perspective of the waterfall and the river. The trails are surrounded by dense tropical foliage, including towering banyan trees, ferns, and a variety of native plants. The lush greenery and the sound of rushing water create a tranquil and refreshing environment.

Rainbow Falls is also a great place for bird watching, as the area is home to several species of native Hawaiian birds. The vibrant flora and fauna add to the overall experience, making it a wonderful destination for nature lovers.

9.   Akaka Falls State Park

Akaka Falls State Park, located on the northeastern Hāmākua Coast of the Big Island of Hawaii, is a gem of natural beauty and a popular destination for visitors seeking to experience one of Hawaii's most stunning waterfalls. The park is named after Akaka Falls, a breathtaking 442-foot waterfall that plunges into a lush, tropical gorge. The park offers visitors an easy and enjoyable way to experience the natural splendor of the island's rainforest environment.

The journey to Akaka Falls is part of the adventure. A paved, 0.4-mile loop trail takes visitors through a dense jungle landscape, filled with bamboo groves, wild orchids, and draping ferns. The trail is well-maintained and suitable for visitors of all ages and fitness levels, making it a perfect family outing. Along the way, the sound of chirping birds and the rustle of leaves in the breeze enhance the immersive experience.

As visitors approach the viewing area for Akaka Falls, the sight of the waterfall becomes awe-inspiring. The water cascades down a sheer cliff face into a pool below, surrounded by lush vegetation. The mist created by the falling water often catches the sunlight, creating a mesmerizing display of rainbows. The viewing platform provides a perfect vantage point for photography, allowing visitors to capture the waterfall in all its glory.

In addition to Akaka Falls, the park features Kahuna Falls, another beautiful waterfall that is visible from a different section of the trail. Though not as tall as Akaka Falls, Kahuna Falls is equally captivating and adds to the overall appeal of the park. The combination of these two waterfalls makes Akaka Falls State Park a must-visit destination for nature enthusiasts and photographers.

The park's flora is another highlight. The diverse plant life includes native Hawaiian species as well as exotic plants introduced to the island. Visitors can see various types of ferns, including the giant hapu'u fern, as well as vibrant hibiscus flowers and ti plants. The rich biodiversity of the park's ecosystem provides an excellent opportunity for botanical exploration and appreciation.

10.   Mauna Kea Summit

The Mauna Kea Summit, located on the Big Island of Hawaii, stands as one of the most extraordinary and awe-inspiring destinations in the world. Rising to an elevation of 13,796 feet above sea level, Mauna Kea is the highest point in Hawaii and, when measured from its base on the ocean floor, the tallest mountain on Earth. This dormant volcano is not only a natural wonder but also a place of profound cultural and scientific significance.

The journey to the summit of Mauna Kea is an adventure in itself. The ascent begins from the Visitor Information Station at an elevation of 9,200 feet, where visitors can acclimate to the high altitude. From there, a rugged, unpaved road leads to the summit. Due to the challenging conditions and the need for four-wheel drive vehicles, it is recommended to take guided tours or heed all safety advice if attempting the drive independently.

Upon reaching the summit, visitors are rewarded with panoramic views that stretch across the island and beyond. The barren, lunar-like landscape is dotted with massive observatories, which take advantage of the summit's exceptional conditions for astronomical observations. The dry, clear air and minimal light pollution make Mauna Kea one of the best places on Earth for stargazing.

The Mauna Kea Observatories, operated by various international institutions, include some of the world's largest and most advanced telescopes. While the observatories themselves are generally not open to the public, their presence underscores the summit's importance to global astronomical research. The Mauna Kea Visitor Information Station offers nightly stargazing programs with telescopes and expert guides, providing a rare opportunity to view celestial wonders from this prime location.

Mauna Kea holds deep cultural significance for Native Hawaiians. The summit is considered sacred, believed to be the dwelling place of the gods and the origin of Hawaiian cosmology. The mountain is home to numerous archaeological sites, including ancient shrines and burial sites, which highlight its spiritual importance. Visitors are encouraged to show respect for the cultural heritage of Mauna Kea by following guidelines and understanding the mountain's sacred status.

11.   Waipio Valley Lookout

Waipio Valley Lookout, located on the northern coast of the Big Island of Hawaii, offers one of the most breathtaking and iconic vistas in the Hawaiian Islands. Known as the "Valley of the Kings," Waipio Valley is steeped in cultural significance and natural beauty, making it a must-visit destination for those seeking to experience the essence of Hawaii.

The lookout provides a stunning panoramic view of Waipio Valley, with its lush green cliffs, black sand beach, and meandering river. The valley is approximately one mile wide and six miles deep, surrounded by steep, verdant walls that rise up to 2,000 feet. This dramatic landscape is not only visually striking but also rich in history and legend.

Waipio Valley holds a special place in Hawaiian culture and history. It was once the residence of Hawaiian royalty and a center of political and religious life. The valley is home to numerous heiau (ancient Hawaiian temples) and other archaeological sites that reflect its historical importance. The fertile land and abundant water supply made it an ideal location for taro cultivation, a staple crop in traditional Hawaiian agriculture.

The lookout is easily accessible by car, with a paved parking area and facilities for visitors. The view from the lookout is spectacular, especially in the early morning or late afternoon when the light creates a magical atmosphere. The sight of the black sand beach contrasting with the blue ocean and the lush greenery of the valley is truly unforgettable.

For the more adventurous, Waipio Valley can be explored further by hiking or horseback riding. The descent into the valley is steep and challenging, with a narrow, winding road that requires caution and a four-wheel-drive vehicle. Once in the valley, visitors can follow trails that lead to the beach, the river, and the waterfalls. The hike to Hi'ilawe Falls, one of the tallest waterfalls in Hawaii, is particularly rewarding, offering an up-close experience of the valley's natural beauty.

12.   Mauna Kea Beach

Mauna Kea Beach, also known as Kauna'oa Beach, is a pristine and picturesque beach located on the Kohala Coast of the Big Island of Hawaii. Renowned for its soft white sand, crystal-clear turquoise waters, and idyllic setting, Mauna Kea Beach is often considered one of the most beautiful beaches in Hawaii.

The beach is situated in front of the Mauna Kea Beach Hotel, which was developed by Laurance S. Rockefeller in the 1960s. The hotel's elegant design and commitment to preserving the natural beauty of the area have made it a landmark on the Kohala Coast. The beach itself is open to the public, and access is provided through a limited number of public parking spaces at the hotel.

One of the most striking features of Mauna Kea Beach is its crescent-shaped shoreline, which gently curves around the bay, creating a sheltered and calm swimming area. The fine white sand and the gradual slope into the water make it an ideal spot for families with children and for those who enjoy wading in the surf. The clear, calm waters are perfect for swimming, snorkeling, and paddleboarding.

Snorkeling at Mauna Kea Beach is particularly rewarding, as the coral reefs just offshore are home to a variety of marine life. Colorful fish, sea turtles, and occasionally manta rays can be spotted in the waters around the reef. The visibility is usually excellent, allowing snorkelers to fully appreciate the underwater beauty.

In addition to swimming and snorkeling, Mauna Kea Beach offers opportunities for other beach activities such as sunbathing, beachcombing, and kayaking. The gentle waves and scenic surroundings create a relaxing and enjoyable environment for visitors looking to unwind and soak up the sun.

The beach is also a fantastic spot for watching the sunset. As the sun dips below the horizon, the sky is painted with hues of orange, pink, and purple, creating a stunning backdrop for an evening stroll along the shore. The tranquil ambiance and natural beauty make Mauna Kea Beach a romantic and serene destination.

13. Hapuna Beach State Recreation Area

Hapuna Beach State Recreation Area, located on the Kohala Coast of the Big Island of Hawaii, is widely celebrated for its expansive white-sand beach and crystal-clear waters. Recognized as one of the best beaches in the United States, Hapuna Beach offers a quintessential tropical paradise experience for visitors seeking sun, sea, and sand.

Stretching nearly half a mile, Hapuna Beach is the largest of the island's white-sand beaches. Its soft, powdery sand and gentle slope into the turquoise ocean make it an ideal spot for swimming, sunbathing, and beachcombing. The beach's broad, open shoreline provides ample space for visitors to spread out and enjoy the serene surroundings.

One of the highlights of Hapuna Beach is its excellent conditions for water activities. The calm, clear waters are perfect for swimming and snorkeling, especially during the summer months when the ocean is typically calm. Snorkelers can explore the vibrant underwater world just offshore, where colorful fish and coral formations are abundant. For those looking to try something different, bodyboarding and paddleboarding are popular activities here, with rental equipment readily available.

Safety is a priority at Hapuna Beach, with lifeguards on duty during the day. This makes it a family-friendly destination where parents can feel comfortable letting their children play in the water. The beach also features amenities such as picnic pavilions, barbecue grills, restrooms, and showers, making it easy for visitors to spend an entire day enjoying the area.

The park surrounding Hapuna Beach is a scenic blend of coastal vegetation and rolling hills, offering several hiking trails that provide stunning views of the coastline and the Pacific Ocean. One of the most popular trails is the Ala Kahakai National Historic Trail, which connects Hapuna Beach to nearby Waialea Bay, another beautiful beach worth exploring. This trail offers hikers a chance to experience the natural beauty and historical significance of the Kohala Coast.

14.   Waikoloa Beach Resort

Waikoloa Beach Resort, located on the sunny Kohala Coast of the Big Island of Hawaii, is a premier vacation destination that offers a blend of luxury, natural beauty, and cultural experiences. This expansive resort area spans over 1,350 acres and is home to world-class accommodations, championship golf courses, high-end shopping, fine dining, and a variety of recreational activities, making it an ideal spot for visitors seeking a luxurious Hawaiian getaway.

The resort area is centered around two main hotel properties: the Hilton Waikoloa Village and the Waikoloa Beach Marriott Resort & Spa. Both of these hotels offer stunning oceanfront views, luxurious accommodations, and a wide range of amenities, including pools, spas, and direct access to beautiful beaches. Guests can enjoy a relaxing stay while being pampered with top-notch service and facilities.

One of the key attractions of Waikoloa Beach Resort is its two championship golf courses: the Waikoloa Beach Course and the Waikoloa Kings' Course. Designed by renowned architects, these courses offer challenging layouts set against the backdrop of lava fields, ocean views, and lush landscapes. Golf enthusiasts from around the world come to play on these pristine courses and enjoy the unique golfing experience they provide.

For those interested in shopping and dining, the resort's two main shopping centers, Kings' Shops and Queens' MarketPlace, offer a diverse selection of stores and restaurants. Visitors can find everything from high-end boutiques and local crafts to gourmet dining and casual eateries. The shopping centers also host regular cultural events, live music, and hula performances, providing a taste of Hawaiian culture and entertainment.

Waikoloa Beach Resort is also known for its beautiful beaches and outdoor activities. Anaehoomalu Bay, often referred to as A-Bay, is a popular spot for sunbathing, swimming, and snorkeling. The calm waters and sandy shore make it an ideal location for families and water sports enthusiasts. The resort offers various water activities, including paddleboarding, kayaking, and sailing.

15.   Kona Coffee Living History Farm

The Kona Coffee Living History Farm, located in Captain Cook on the Big Island of Hawaii, offers a unique and immersive experience that transports visitors back to the early 20th century to explore the rich history of coffee farming in the region. Operated by the Kona Historical Society, this living history museum is the only one of its kind dedicated to preserving the heritage of Kona coffee farming, providing a fascinating glimpse into the daily lives of the farmers who have cultivated this world-renowned crop.

Established in the 1920s, the farm is a well-preserved example of a typical family-operated coffee farm from that era. Visitors are greeted by costumed interpreters who portray the farm's original Japanese owners and workers, providing authentic insights into their lives and work. These interpreters demonstrate traditional farming techniques, from coffee cherry picking and processing to roasting and brewing, allowing visitors to experience firsthand the labor-intensive process of producing Kona coffee.

One of the highlights of the Kona Coffee Living History Farm is the opportunity to explore the historic farmhouse and outbuildings. The farmhouse is furnished with period-appropriate items, offering a snapshot of domestic life in the early 20th century. Visitors can see the kitchen, living areas, and sleeping quarters, all meticulously maintained to reflect the lifestyle of the time. The farm also includes a traditional Japanese bathhouse, a chicken coop, and a mule-driven mill, each adding to the authentic historical atmosphere.

The farm's orchards are another key feature, with rows of coffee trees showcasing the different stages of growth and production. Visitors can participate in hands-on activities such as picking coffee cherries and learning about the pruning and care of the trees. The farm also grows other crops typical of the period, including macadamia nuts, avocados, and tropical fruits, highlighting the diversified nature of farming in Kona.

Throughout the visit, guests are encouraged to interact with the interpreters, ask questions, and engage in the daily activities of the farm. This interactive approach not only makes the visit educational but also deeply engaging, providing a memorable experience for visitors of all ages.

16.   Kealakekua Bay

Kealakekua Bay, located on the western coast of the Big Island of Hawaii, is a place of stunning natural beauty and significant historical importance. This marine sanctuary, known for its crystal-clear waters and vibrant coral reefs, offers visitors a chance to explore one of Hawaii's most pristine underwater environments while also connecting with the island's rich history.

The bay is perhaps best known as the site where British explorer Captain James Cook first landed in Hawaii in 1779. A white obelisk on the northern shore of the bay marks the spot where Cook was killed in a conflict with Native Hawaiians. This monument, accessible only by boat or a strenuous hike, stands as a historical landmark commemorating Cook's arrival and his subsequent impact on Hawaiian history.

Kealakekua Bay is a popular destination for snorkeling and diving, thanks to its exceptionally clear waters and abundant marine life. The bay is home to a diverse array of fish, sea turtles, dolphins, and vibrant coral reefs. The calm waters and excellent visibility make it an ideal spot for both beginners and experienced snorkelers. The area around the Captain Cook Monument is particularly renowned for its underwater scenery, with large schools of tropical fish and intricate coral formations.

For those interested in exploring the bay, there are several ways to access its waters. Kayaking is a popular choice, with rentals available from local operators who provide guided tours and equipment. Paddling across the bay offers a unique perspective of its scenic beauty and the opportunity to reach otherwise inaccessible areas. Snorkeling tours by boat are also available, often combining snorkeling with dolphin watching, as spinner dolphins frequently visit the bay.

The historical and cultural significance of Kealakekua Bay extends beyond Captain Cook. The bay and its surrounding areas are rich with archaeological sites, including ancient temples (heiau), burial caves, and rock carvings (petroglyphs). These sites provide a window into the lives of the Native Hawaiians who inhabited the region long before European contact. Guided tours and educational programs are available for those interested in learning more about the bay's cultural heritage.

Pu'uhonua o Honaunau National Historical Park, located on the western coast of the Big Island of Hawaii, is a place of deep historical and cultural significance. This 420-acre park preserves and interprets the traditional Hawaiian place of refuge, or pu'uhonua, which was a sanctuary for those who had broken ancient laws (kapu) and sought absolution. The park offers a unique glimpse into Hawaii's ancient past, its traditions, and its complex societal structure.

The centerpiece of Pu'uhonua o Honaunau is the pu'uhonua itself, a sacred site that provided a place of safety and forgiveness. Under the ancient Hawaiian legal system, strict laws governed every aspect of society, and breaking these laws often resulted in severe punishment or death. However, if offenders could reach a pu'uhonua, they would be absolved by a priest and allowed to return to society without fear of retribution. This aspect of the park highlights the sophisticated legal and religious systems that existed in pre-contact Hawaii.

Visitors to the park can explore a variety of well-preserved archaeological sites that tell the story of Hawaii's ancient culture. The Great Wall, a massive structure over 10 feet high and 17 feet thick, delineates the boundary of the pu'uhonua. Constructed from lava rock without the use of mortar, this impressive feat of engineering stands as a testament to the skills of ancient Hawaiian builders.

Adjacent to the pu'uhonua is the royal grounds, an area that was once the residence of Hawaiian chiefs. Here, visitors can see reconstructed thatched hale (houses), including the hale o keawe, a temple that once housed the bones of deified chiefs, believed to possess great spiritual power (mana). The presence of these bones added to the sanctity and protective aura of the pu'uhonua.

The park also features a variety of other cultural and historical landmarks, such as fishponds (loko i'a), used for aquaculture, and the Keone'ele Cove, a royal canoe landing area. The grounds are scattered with petroglyphs and carved wooden images known as ki'i, which provide further insight into the religious and artistic practices of the time.

18.   Mauna Loa Observatory

Mauna Loa Observatory, situated at an elevation of 11,135 feet on the northern flank of Mauna Loa volcano on the Big Island of Hawaii, is a premier research facility dedicated to monitoring and understanding atmospheric conditions. Operated by the National Oceanic and Atmospheric Administration (NOAA), this remote observatory plays a critical role in global climate science and has been at the forefront of atmospheric research since its establishment in 1956.

The observatory's primary mission is to collect long-term data on atmospheric gases, including carbon dioxide (CO_2), methane (CH_4), and other greenhouse gases. The Mauna Loa Observatory is particularly renowned for its continuous record of CO_2 measurements, known as the Keeling Curve. Named after Dr. Charles David Keeling, who initiated the measurements, the Keeling Curve is a graph that shows the ongoing change in the concentration of carbon dioxide in Earth's atmosphere since the late 1950s. This data has been crucial in demonstrating the rapid increase in CO_2 levels and its link to human activities, significantly contributing to our understanding of global climate change.

The location of Mauna Loa Observatory is ideal for atmospheric measurements due to its high altitude, remote location, and minimal influence from local pollution sources. These factors ensure that the air sampled at the observatory is representative of the broader atmosphere, providing accurate and reliable data. The observatory's isolated position also means it experiences minimal light and noise pollution, which is advantageous for various types of atmospheric observations and experiments.

In addition to greenhouse gas monitoring, Mauna Loa Observatory conducts a wide range of atmospheric research. This includes tracking aerosols, solar radiation, ozone levels, and other atmospheric constituents. The data collected is used to study climate dynamics, atmospheric chemistry, and the effects of pollutants on air quality and climate. These studies are essential for developing climate models and for informing environmental policy and regulation.

Kauai

1.   Waimea Canyon State Park

Waimea Canyon State Park, located on the western side of the island of Kauai in Hawaii, is often referred to as the "Grand Canyon of the Pacific." This awe-inspiring natural wonder stretches approximately 14 miles long, one mile wide, and more than 3,600 feet deep, offering visitors breathtaking vistas and a dramatic landscape of red rock cliffs, deep gorges, and lush valleys.

The canyon was formed by the Waimea River and the island's volcanic activity, which have sculpted its rugged terrain over millions of years. The result is a stunning display of geological history, with layers of red, brown, and green rock that change color with the shifting sunlight. The canyon's unique beauty is further enhanced by the lush vegetation and waterfalls that dot the landscape, creating a vivid contrast against the rocky cliffs.

Visitors to Waimea Canyon State Park can enjoy a variety of activities, including hiking, sightseeing, and photography. The park offers several lookout points, such as the popular Waimea Canyon Overlook and the Pu'u Hinahina Lookout, both of which provide panoramic views of the canyon and the surrounding landscape. These lookout points are easily accessible by car and offer excellent opportunities for capturing the canyon's grandeur on camera.

For those seeking a more immersive experience, the park features a network of hiking trails that cater to various skill levels. The Canyon Trail, for example, is a moderate hike that leads to the spectacular Waipo'o Falls, a two-tiered waterfall that plunges into the canyon. Along the trails, hikers can observe native plant species, birds, and occasionally, mountain goats.

Waimea Canyon State Park is also known for its rich cultural history. The area was historically significant to the native Hawaiian people, who considered it a sacred place. Interpretive signs throughout the park provide information about the canyon's geological and cultural significance, offering visitors a deeper understanding of this remarkable landscape.

2. Na Pali Coast State Wilderness Park

Na Pali Coast State Wilderness Park, located on the northwest coast of Kauai, is one of Hawaii's most iconic and visually stunning natural areas. Spanning over 6,175 acres, the park is renowned for its dramatic cliffs, lush valleys, cascading waterfalls, and pristine beaches. The Na Pali Coast is accessible primarily by boat, helicopter, or via the challenging Kalalau Trail, which traverses the coastline.

The park's landscape is characterized by its steep, emerald-green cliffs that rise up to 4,000 feet above the Pacific Ocean. These cliffs, or "pali," are interspersed with narrow valleys and numerous waterfalls, creating a breathtaking and rugged terrain. The coastline's inaccessibility by road has preserved its natural beauty, making it a haven for outdoor enthusiasts and adventure seekers.

One of the best ways to experience the Na Pali Coast is by taking a boat tour. These tours offer an up-close view of the towering cliffs, sea caves, and marine life, including dolphins, sea turtles, and humpback whales. For a bird's-eye perspective, helicopter tours provide a spectacular overview of the entire coastline, revealing hidden valleys and waterfalls that are otherwise inaccessible.

For those seeking a more immersive adventure, hiking the Kalalau Trail is a must. This 11-mile trail begins at Ke'e Beach and winds along the coast to Kalalau Beach. The trail is known for its challenging terrain, with steep ascents and descents, narrow paths, and stunning views at every turn. Hikers are rewarded with some of the most scenic vistas in Hawaii, including the verdant Hanakapiai Valley and the secluded Kalalau Beach, where camping is permitted with a permit.

The Na Pali Coast is also rich in cultural history. Ancient Hawaiians once lived and farmed in the fertile valleys, leaving behind archaeological sites such as heiau (temples), agricultural terraces, and rock walls. The park's preservation efforts help protect these cultural resources, allowing visitors to appreciate the area's historical significance alongside its natural beauty.

3.   Kalalau Trail

The Kalalau Trail, located on the Na Pali Coast of Kauai, is one of Hawaii's most famous and challenging hikes. This 11-mile trail offers intrepid hikers an unforgettable journey through some of the most stunning and rugged terrain in the Hawaiian Islands. Beginning at Ke'e Beach and ending at the secluded Kalalau Beach, the trail provides access to breathtaking vistas, lush valleys, and pristine beaches.

The trail is renowned for its difficulty, with steep inclines, narrow paths, and numerous stream crossings. Hikers must be prepared for a physically demanding trek that requires careful planning and respect for the elements. However, those who undertake the journey are rewarded with some of the most spectacular scenery in Hawaii.

The first two miles of the trail lead to Hanakapiai Beach, a popular day hike destination. This section of the trail offers stunning views of the Na Pali Coast and lush tropical vegetation. Upon reaching Hanakapiai Beach, hikers can choose to explore the Hanakapiai Falls, an additional two-mile hike inland that leads to a majestic 300-foot waterfall.

Beyond Hanakapiai Beach, the trail becomes more challenging as it continues along the coastline. The path winds through the verdant Hanakoa Valley, where hikers can find a designated camping area. The trail's final stretch involves navigating the steep and narrow paths of "Crawler's Ledge," a section that requires sure-footedness and caution due to its exposure and drop-offs.

The ultimate reward for completing the Kalalau Trail is arriving at Kalalau Beach, a remote and idyllic beach surrounded by towering cliffs and lush vegetation. The beach is a perfect spot for camping, swimming, and exploring sea caves. Camping permits are required and must be obtained in advance from the Hawaii Department of Land and Natural Resources.

Hiking the Kalalau Trail is not just a physical challenge but also a spiritual journey. The trail passes through ancient Hawaiian lands, with remnants of agricultural terraces and sacred sites visible along the way. Hikers often feel a deep connection to the land and its history, adding a profound cultural dimension to their adventure.

4.   Hanakapiai Falls

Hanakapiai Falls, located on the Na Pali Coast of Kauai, is a spectacular 300-foot waterfall that attracts hikers and nature enthusiasts seeking a challenging and rewarding adventure. The journey to the falls begins at Ke'e Beach, following the Kalalau Trail for the first two miles to Hanakapiai Beach, and then continuing another two miles inland to reach the falls. This four-mile hike (eight miles round trip) offers stunning scenery and a glimpse into the rugged beauty of the Na Pali Coast.

The initial section of the hike from Ke'e Beach to Hanakapiai Beach is a popular day hike. This part of the trail winds along the coast, providing breathtaking views of the ocean, towering cliffs, and lush vegetation. The path is relatively well-maintained but can be steep and slippery in places, especially after rain. Hikers are rewarded with the sight of Hanakapiai Beach, a picturesque spot where the Hanakapiai Stream meets the ocean. While the beach is beautiful, it is not safe for swimming due to strong currents and rip tides.

From Hanakapiai Beach, the trail to Hanakapiai Falls becomes more challenging. The path follows the Hanakapiai Stream, crossing it several times. Hikers should be prepared for uneven terrain, muddy conditions, and potential stream crossings that can be tricky after heavy rainfall. The lush rainforest surroundings, filled with bamboo groves, tropical flowers, and a variety of native plants, create a serene and immersive experience.

As hikers approach Hanakapiai Falls, the sound of rushing water grows louder, and the sight of the cascading waterfall emerges through the foliage. The falls plunge 300 feet into a clear pool, surrounded by moss-covered rocks and vibrant greenery. The area around the falls is an ideal spot for a refreshing swim or simply relaxing and enjoying the natural beauty. The cool, pristine waters provide a welcome respite after the challenging hike.

Hanakapiai Falls is not only a natural wonder but also a place of cultural significance. The Hanakapiai Valley was once home to Native Hawaiian communities who farmed taro and other crops in the fertile soil. Hikers can still see remnants of ancient agricultural terraces and rock walls along the trail, offering a glimpse into the island's historical and cultural heritage.

5.   Limahuli Garden and Preserve

Limahuli Garden and Preserve, located on the lush north shore of Kauai, Hawaii, is a stunning botanical garden and conservation area dedicated to preserving native Hawaiian plants and traditional agricultural practices. Spread over 1,000 acres, this extraordinary site offers a unique blend of natural beauty, cultural heritage, and scientific research.

The garden is part of the National Tropical Botanical Garden network and serves as a living laboratory for the conservation of rare and endangered Hawaiian plant species. Visitors to Limahuli Garden can explore a diverse array of plant life, from ancient taro terraces (loʻi) that date back over 700 years to modern conservation efforts that protect native flora. The garden's layout reflects traditional Hawaiian land management practices, known as ahupuaʻa, which divide the land into sections from the mountains to the sea, ensuring sustainable resource use.

A guided or self-guided tour through Limahuli Garden provides an educational and immersive experience. Visitors can learn about the significance of various plants in Hawaiian culture, including their uses in medicine, food, and daily life. The garden's interpretive signs and knowledgeable guides offer insights into the ecological and cultural importance of the plants and the traditional practices used to cultivate them.

The preserve's breathtaking landscape includes cascading waterfalls, verdant valleys, and panoramic views of the Pacific Ocean. The pristine setting is home to numerous native birds, insects, and other wildlife, making it a haven for nature enthusiasts and photographers. The garden's trails are well-maintained and offer varying levels of difficulty, accommodating both casual walkers and avid hikers.

Limahuli Garden and Preserve is more than just a botanical garden; it is a place of cultural preservation and environmental stewardship. By showcasing the rich biodiversity and traditional knowledge of Hawaii, the garden plays a vital role in educating the public about the importance of conservation and the interconnectedness of culture and nature.

6.   Tunnels Beach

Tunnels Beach, known locally as Makua Beach, is a breathtaking destination on Kauai's north shore, renowned for its pristine sands, crystal-clear waters, and exceptional snorkeling and diving opportunities. Nestled against the dramatic backdrop of lush green mountains and jagged cliffs, Tunnels Beach is a paradise for outdoor enthusiasts and beachgoers alike.

The beach gets its name from the underwater lava tubes and caverns that create a labyrinthine underwater landscape, making it a premier spot for snorkeling and scuba diving. The reef at Tunnels Beach is extensive and teeming with marine life, including colorful coral formations, tropical fish, sea turtles, and occasionally monk seals. The shallow inner reef is perfect for beginner snorkelers, while the deeper outer reef attracts more experienced divers looking to explore the underwater tunnels and caves.

Tunnels Beach offers a tranquil and uncrowded atmosphere, making it an ideal location for sunbathing, swimming, and picnicking. The beach's golden sands are soft and inviting, and the gentle waves of the inner reef create a safe environment for families with children. The beach is also popular among surfers, particularly during the winter months when the surf can be more challenging.

The scenic beauty of Tunnels Beach extends beyond its shoreline. The surrounding area is lush with tropical vegetation and offers stunning views of Bali Hai, the iconic mountain made famous by the movie "South Pacific." The sunsets at Tunnels Beach are particularly spectacular, painting the sky with vibrant hues of orange, pink, and purple.

Access to Tunnels Beach is somewhat limited, contributing to its serene and unspoiled charm. Parking can be a challenge, especially during peak times, so visitors are advised to arrive early. There are no facilities such as restrooms or showers at the beach, so it's important to come prepared with all necessary supplies, including water, snacks, and sun protection.

7.   Hanalei Bay

Hanalei Bay, located on the north shore of Kauai, is a stunning crescent-shaped bay known for its two-mile stretch of golden sand, crystal-clear waters, and lush mountain backdrop. This picturesque destination is a favorite among locals and visitors alike, offering a perfect blend of natural beauty, recreational activities, and a laid-back Hawaiian atmosphere.

The bay's calm waters and gentle waves make it an ideal spot for swimming, paddleboarding, and kayaking. During the summer months, the bay's tranquil conditions are perfect for families with children and those looking to enjoy a relaxing day at the beach. In the winter, the waves become more powerful, attracting surfers from around the world who come to ride the impressive swells.

One of the iconic features of Hanalei Bay is the Hanalei Pier, a historic structure that extends into the bay and offers a popular spot for fishing, jumping into the water, or simply taking in the panoramic views. The pier's rustic charm adds to the bay's appeal and serves as a reminder of Kauai's rich history and cultural heritage.

The surrounding town of Hanalei complements the bay's natural beauty with its charming, laid-back vibe. The town is home to an array of shops, restaurants, and art galleries, providing visitors with plenty of options for dining, shopping, and exploring local culture. From casual eateries serving fresh fish tacos to upscale restaurants offering gourmet Hawaiian cuisine, Hanalei has something to satisfy every palate.

Outdoor enthusiasts will find plenty of opportunities for adventure around Hanalei Bay. The nearby Hanalei River offers scenic kayaking and paddleboarding experiences, with lush greenery and mountain views along the way. Hiking trails in the area, such as the Okolehao Trail, provide stunning vistas of the bay and the surrounding valley, rewarding hikers with breathtaking scenery.

Hanalei Bay's stunning landscape has also made it a popular location for film and television. Its natural beauty has been featured in numerous movies, enhancing its reputation as one of Hawaii's most picturesque destinations.

8.   Queen's Bath

Queen's Bath, located on the north shore of Kauai in the town of Princeville, is a unique and natural tidal pool carved into the lava rock. This geological wonder is known for its striking beauty and the opportunity it provides for visitors to swim and relax in a natural setting, surrounded by the rugged coastline and the crashing waves of the Pacific Ocean.

The pool gets its name from being a place where Hawaiian royalty once bathed, reflecting its serene and majestic qualities. During the summer months, when the ocean is calm, Queen's Bath offers a tranquil and picturesque spot for swimming. The clear, turquoise waters of the pool are refreshed with each wave, maintaining a cool and inviting environment. Snorkeling in Queen's Bath can also be a delightful experience, as the pool is home to various small fish and other marine life.

To reach Queen's Bath, visitors must hike a short but steep trail from a residential area in Princeville. The trail can be muddy and slippery, especially after rain, so proper footwear is recommended. The hike takes visitors through lush vegetation and down to the rocky shoreline, where the pool is located. The scenery along the trail and at the pool is breathtaking, offering stunning views of the ocean and the surrounding cliffs.

However, Queen's Bath can be dangerous, particularly during the winter months when the surf is high. Strong waves and unpredictable ocean conditions can make swimming hazardous, and several accidents have occurred over the years. Visitors are strongly advised to exercise caution, heed posted warnings, and avoid the pool during rough seas.

Despite the risks, Queen's Bath remains a popular destination due to its natural beauty and the unique experience it offers. The contrast between the calm waters of the pool and the powerful waves crashing against the rocks creates a dramatic and memorable setting.

For those who visit responsibly and respect the natural conditions, Queen's Bath provides an unparalleled opportunity to enjoy one of Kauai's most distinctive natural features. Whether you're soaking in the pool, exploring the rocky coastline, or simply taking in the spectacular views, Queen's Bath offers a glimpse into the raw and untamed beauty of Hawaii's north shore.

9.   Princeville Botanical Gardens

Princeville Botanical Gardens, located on the north shore of Kauai in the lush community of Princeville, is a family-owned botanical garden that offers visitors a chance to explore a diverse collection of tropical plants and flowers. Spanning eight acres, the gardens are set against the stunning backdrop of Kauai's verdant landscape, providing a serene and educational experience for nature enthusiasts.

The gardens are meticulously designed and maintained, featuring a variety of plant collections that include native Hawaiian species, exotic tropical flowers, medicinal plants, and fruit trees. As visitors meander through the winding paths, they are treated to vibrant displays of orchids, heliconias, bromeliads, and hibiscus, among many others. The garden's layout is thoughtfully curated to highlight the beauty and diversity of the plant kingdom, with each section offering a unique theme and ambiance.

Guided tours are available and highly recommended, as they provide valuable insights into the botanical and cultural significance of the plants. Knowledgeable guides share fascinating stories about the garden's history, the uses of different plants in traditional Hawaiian medicine, and sustainable gardening practices. These tours often include opportunities to taste exotic fruits and homemade chocolate, adding a sensory delight to the botanical experience.

One of the garden's highlights is the extensive collection of cacao trees, which are used to produce small-batch, artisan chocolate. Visitors can learn about the entire process of chocolate making, from harvesting cacao pods to fermenting, drying, and crafting the final product. This immersive experience is a treat for chocolate lovers and offers a deeper appreciation for this beloved delicacy.

Princeville Botanical Gardens also places a strong emphasis on conservation and education. The garden actively participates in efforts to preserve endangered Hawaiian plants and promote environmental stewardship. Educational programs and workshops are offered to engage the community and visitors in sustainable gardening and conservation practices.

10.   Kilauea Lighthouse

Perched on the northernmost tip of Kauai, the Kilauea Lighthouse stands as a historic beacon and a stunning landmark on the island's rugged coastline. Established in 1913, the lighthouse sits on a dramatic bluff overlooking the Pacific Ocean, offering visitors breathtaking panoramic views and a glimpse into Hawaii's maritime history.

The Kilauea Lighthouse is part of the Kilauea Point National Wildlife Refuge, a protected area that serves as a sanctuary for a variety of seabirds and other wildlife. The refuge is home to species such as the Laysan albatross, red-footed boobies, and the Hawaiian monk seal. Birdwatchers and nature enthusiasts will find the area particularly rewarding, as the high cliffs provide excellent vantage points for observing these birds in their natural habitat.

The lighthouse itself is a marvel of early 20th-century engineering. Standing 52 feet tall, it was originally equipped with a powerful Fresnel lens, which projected its beam up to 20 miles out to sea, guiding ships safely along the treacherous coast. Today, the lighthouse is no longer operational but has been preserved as a historical monument, providing insight into the island's navigational history and the vital role the lighthouse played in maritime safety.

Visitors to Kilauea Lighthouse can explore the surrounding wildlife refuge and enjoy the scenic trails that offer spectacular views of the ocean and the rugged coastline. Informational plaques along the paths provide details about the local flora, fauna, and the history of the lighthouse. Guided tours are available, offering a deeper understanding of the area's natural and historical significance.

The lighthouse grounds also feature a visitor center and gift shop, where guests can learn more about the refuge's conservation efforts and purchase souvenirs. The visitor center often hosts educational programs and events, making it a great place for families and school groups to learn about Hawaii's unique ecosystems and conservation challenges.

11.   Moloa'a Bay

Moloa'a Bay, located on the northeastern shore of Kauai, is a picturesque and secluded beach that offers a tranquil escape from the more crowded tourist spots on the island. Known for its crescent-shaped white sand beach, clear turquoise waters, and lush surrounding vegetation, Moloa'a Bay is a hidden gem that embodies the natural beauty of Kauai.

The bay's calm and clear waters make it an excellent spot for swimming, snorkeling, and paddleboarding. The gentle waves and sandy bottom create a safe environment for families and children, while the rocky outcrops on either end of the bay provide excellent snorkeling opportunities. The underwater world of Moloa'a Bay is teeming with colorful fish, vibrant coral, and other marine life, making it a delightful destination for snorkelers of all skill levels.

The beach at Moloa'a Bay is framed by verdant hills and coconut palms, creating a scenic and serene backdrop. The bay's relatively remote location means it is often less crowded than other beaches on Kauai, allowing visitors to enjoy a more peaceful and intimate experience. It's an ideal spot for sunbathing, picnicking, and simply soaking in the natural beauty of the island.

Access to Moloa'a Bay requires a short walk from the parking area through a lush tropical landscape, adding to the sense of adventure and seclusion. The path is relatively easy to navigate, and the reward is a pristine and uncrowded beach that feels like a private paradise.

In addition to its natural charm, Moloa'a Bay holds a bit of pop culture trivia. It was the filming location for the pilot episode of the classic TV show "Gilligan's Island," adding a touch of nostalgia for fans of the series.

Visitors to Moloa'a Bay are encouraged to respect the natural environment and local customs. There are no facilities such as restrooms or showers at the beach, so it is important to come prepared with all necessary supplies, including water, snacks, and sun protection.

Moloa'a Bay is a perfect destination for those seeking a quiet and beautiful beach experience on Kauai. Its combination of crystal-clear waters, scenic surroundings, and tranquil atmosphere make it a must-visit spot for nature lovers and beachgoers looking to escape the hustle and bustle of more popular tourist areas.

12.   Smith's Tropical Paradise

Smith's Tropical Paradise, located along the Wailua River on the east side of Kauai, is a lush 30-acre botanical and cultural garden that offers visitors a captivating blend of natural beauty and Hawaiian heritage. Operated by the Smith family for over 50 years, this tropical oasis provides a serene setting to explore a wide variety of plants, enjoy cultural performances, and experience a traditional Hawaiian luau.

The garden is meticulously landscaped, featuring meandering pathways that lead through diverse sections showcasing exotic flowers, towering palms, fruit trees, and serene lagoons. Visitors can stroll at their own pace, taking in the vibrant colors and fragrances of the tropical flora. The gardens are home to over 20 varieties of fruit, including mango, papaya, and starfruit, as well as numerous species of orchids, hibiscus, and heliconias.

One of the highlights of Smith's Tropical Paradise is the evening luau, a traditional Hawaiian feast accompanied by live music, hula dancing, and a dramatic torch-lit performance. The luau begins with an imu ceremony, where guests can witness the unearthing of the kalua pig that has been slow-cooked in an underground oven. The feast includes a buffet of Hawaiian and local dishes, such as poi, lomi-lomi salmon, and fresh island fish, providing a delicious and authentic taste of Hawaiian cuisine.

In addition to the luau, Smith's Tropical Paradise offers a variety of cultural activities and performances throughout the day. Guests can enjoy traditional Hawaiian music, hula lessons, and craft demonstrations, gaining a deeper appreciation for the island's rich cultural heritage. The gardens also feature replicas of ancient Polynesian and Filipino village sites, providing insights into the diverse cultures that have influenced Hawaii over the centuries.

Another unique attraction at Smith's Tropical Paradise is the Fern Grotto boat tour. Departing from the gardens, the boat tour takes visitors up the Wailua River to the famous Fern Grotto, a natural lava rock cave draped with ferns. The grotto is a popular spot for weddings and is known for its stunning natural acoustics. During the tour, guides share the history and legends of the area, enhancing the overall experience.

13.   Fern Grotto

The Fern Grotto, located on the east side of Kauai along the Wailua River, is a lush, natural amphitheater famous for its verdant canopy of ferns and unique acoustics. This botanical marvel is accessible only by boat, adding to the sense of adventure and exclusivity that surrounds a visit to this picturesque spot.

The journey to Fern Grotto begins with a leisurely boat ride along the tranquil Wailua River, the only navigable river in Hawaii. The boat tour, often accompanied by live Hawaiian music and hula dancing, offers scenic views of the surrounding tropical landscape. Guides typically share stories and legends of the area, enriching the experience with cultural and historical context.

Upon arrival, visitors disembark and walk a short distance through a tropical rainforest to reach the grotto. The grotto itself is a natural lava rock cave, overgrown with lush green ferns that cascade down from the ceiling, creating a stunning visual effect. The combination of the cave's natural formation and the dense fern growth provides a serene and almost magical atmosphere.

One of the highlights of visiting Fern Grotto is its remarkable acoustics. The grotto is often used for weddings and other ceremonies, with the natural acoustics amplifying the voices and music beautifully. Visitors are often treated to a live performance of the Hawaiian Wedding Song, adding to the romantic and enchanting ambiance of the location.

The Fern Grotto is not just a natural wonder but also a place of cultural significance. It has been a sacred site for Native Hawaiians for centuries, used for religious and ceremonial purposes. Today, it continues to be a popular location for weddings and other special events, drawing visitors who seek to experience its unique beauty and tranquility.

Overall, a visit to Fern Grotto offers a combination of natural beauty, cultural history, and a touch of adventure. The boat ride along the Wailua River, the lush surroundings, and the serene atmosphere of the grotto make it a must-see destination for anyone visiting Kauai.

14.   Wailua River State Park

Wailua River State Park, located on the east side of Kauai, is a stunning natural area that encompasses the only navigable river in Hawaii, the Wailua River. The park is renowned for its lush landscapes, historical significance, and recreational opportunities, making it a popular destination for both tourists and locals.

The Wailua River meanders through the park, offering a serene setting for various water activities such as kayaking, paddleboarding, and boat tours. The calm, navigable waters make it an ideal spot for these activities, allowing visitors to explore the river at their own pace while taking in the surrounding tropical scenery. The river is flanked by verdant rainforests, towering coconut trees, and scenic waterfalls, providing a picturesque backdrop for any adventure.

One of the key attractions within Wailua River State Park is the Fern Grotto, a natural lava rock cave covered in lush ferns. Accessible only by boat, the grotto is famous for its unique acoustics and natural beauty. Visitors can take a guided boat tour to the grotto, where they can enjoy live Hawaiian music and learn about the cultural significance of the site.

Another highlight of the park is Wailua Falls, a dramatic double waterfall that cascades into a large pool below. Easily accessible by car, the falls can be viewed from a lookout point, providing a breathtaking sight, especially after a heavy rainfall when the water flow is at its peak. The falls are a favorite spot for photographers and nature enthusiasts.

Wailua River State Park is also rich in cultural and historical sites. The area was once a major center for Native Hawaiian religion and politics, and remnants of this history can be seen throughout the park. Notable sites include the ancient heiau (temples) such as Poliahu Heiau and Holoholokū Heiau, which were significant in the religious and social life of the island's early inhabitants.

For those interested in exploring on foot, the park offers several hiking trails that lead through the lush landscape, providing opportunities to see native plants, birds, and other wildlife. These trails range from easy walks to more challenging hikes, catering to different levels of fitness and experience.

15.   Kauai Museum

Located in the heart of Lihue, the Kauai Museum offers a comprehensive and fascinating glimpse into the rich history and culture of the Garden Isle. Established in 1960, the museum is housed in two historic buildings and features extensive collections that span the island's geological formation, indigenous culture, and more recent history.

The museum's exhibits are thoughtfully curated to provide a chronological journey through Kauai's past. Visitors can start with the geological origins of the island, learning about its volcanic birth and the natural forces that have shaped its stunning landscapes. Detailed displays include information on Kauai's unique flora and fauna, many of which are found nowhere else in the world.

A significant portion of the museum is dedicated to the culture and history of Native Hawaiians. Exhibits feature traditional artifacts such as tools, weapons, clothing, and religious items. The museum also delves into the social and political structures of ancient Hawaiian society, offering insights into the lives of Kauai's early inhabitants. Visitors can learn about the significance of hula, the art of canoe building, and the role of the ali'i (chiefs) in Hawaiian culture.

One of the museum's standout features is its collection of Hawaiian featherwork, known as 'ahu 'ula and mahiole. These intricate capes and helmets, made from the feathers of native birds, were worn by Hawaiian royalty and are a testament to the artistry and craftsmanship of the Hawaiian people.

The museum also covers the period of Western contact and the subsequent changes that occurred on the island. Exhibits highlight the arrival of Captain Cook, the influence of missionaries, and the development of the sugar and pineapple industries that transformed Kauai's economy and landscape.

In addition to its permanent exhibits, the Kauai Museum hosts rotating exhibitions, educational programs, and cultural events throughout the year. These activities aim to engage the local community and visitors alike, fostering a deeper understanding and appreciation of Kauai's heritage.

16.   Makauwahi Cave Reserve

Makauwahi Cave Reserve, located on the south shore of Kauai near the town of Poipu, is a unique and fascinating destination that offers visitors a journey through time. This large limestone cave and sinkhole, the largest of its kind in Hawaii, is an archaeological and paleontological treasure trove, providing invaluable insights into the island's natural and human history.

The reserve covers 17 acres and is centered around the Makauwahi Cave, which was formed by the collapse of a limestone cavern. The cave's floor is a rich deposit of sediment that has preserved a record of the island's environment over the past 10,000 years. These sediments contain fossils, plant remains, and artifacts that tell the story of Kauai's changing climate, ecosystems, and human impact.

Visitors to Makauwahi Cave Reserve can take guided tours that explain the significance of the cave and its findings. The tours are led by knowledgeable guides who share the history of the site, the discoveries made there, and the ongoing research conducted by scientists from around the world. Highlights of the tour include viewing the cave's impressive geological formations and learning about the extinct species that once inhabited the island, such as the flightless Hawaiian rail and giant duck.

The reserve is also a living laboratory for ecological restoration. Efforts are underway to restore native vegetation and reintroduce species that were once common in the area. Visitors can see the results of these efforts in the surrounding landscape, where native plants are thriving once again. The reserve's staff and volunteers work tirelessly to remove invasive species and replant native ones, creating a habitat that resembles what Kauai might have looked like before human arrival.

In addition to its scientific and ecological importance, Makauwahi Cave Reserve offers a variety of recreational opportunities. The reserve features several hiking trails that wind through the restored landscape, offering stunning views of the coast and the chance to see native wildlife. Birdwatchers, in particular, will appreciate the diversity of species that can be spotted in the area.

17.   Maha'ulepu Heritage Trail

The Maha'ulepu Heritage Trail, located on the southern coast of Kauai, is a scenic and culturally rich coastal path that offers hikers stunning ocean views, fascinating geological formations, and a glimpse into the island's natural and historical heritage. Stretching approximately four miles round-trip from Shipwreck Beach to Punahoa Point, the trail provides a moderate hike suitable for all ages and fitness levels.

The trail begins at Shipwreck Beach, named for an old shipwreck that once lay on its shore. From here, hikers are treated to breathtaking views of the rugged coastline, with waves crashing against the rocky cliffs and pristine sandy beaches below. The trail meanders along the coast, passing through diverse landscapes including sandy dunes, limestone formations, and verdant valleys.

One of the highlights of the Maha'ulepu Heritage Trail is the geological diversity on display. Hikers can observe ancient fossilized sand dunes, also known as lithified sand dunes, which have been shaped by wind and water over thousands of years. The limestone formations, interspersed with pockets of native vegetation, add a unique visual appeal to the trail.

In addition to its natural beauty, the trail is rich in cultural history. The area was once a significant site for ancient Hawaiian activities such as fishing, farming, and religious practices. Along the trail, hikers can find remnants of these past activities, including ancient Hawaiian fishponds and agricultural terraces. Interpretive signs provide information about the historical and cultural significance of these sites, enhancing the hiking experience.

Wildlife enthusiasts will appreciate the opportunity to spot various bird species along the trail, including the endangered Hawaiian monk seal, which occasionally basks on the secluded beaches. The coastal waters are also home to sea turtles and, during the winter months, humpback whales can often be seen breaching offshore.

The Maha'ulepu Heritage Trail is not only a hike through beautiful scenery but also a journey through time, offering insights into the natural and cultural history of Kauai.

18.   Poipu Beach Park

Poipu Beach Park, located on the sunny south shore of Kauai, is one of the island's most popular and family-friendly beaches. Known for its golden sands, clear waters, and excellent amenities, Poipu Beach Park offers a perfect destination for swimming, snorkeling, picnicking, and enjoying the natural beauty of Hawaii.

The beach is divided into several sections, each catering to different activities. The eastern side, known as Baby Beach, is a shallow, sheltered area ideal for young children and families. The calm waters and gentle waves make it a safe spot for toddlers to splash and play. Nearby, a natural wading pool formed by a crescent-shaped sandbar provides additional protection from the surf, making it an excellent location for beginner swimmers.

The western side of Poipu Beach is popular for snorkeling and swimming. The clear waters and vibrant coral reefs attract a variety of marine life, including colorful fish, sea turtles, and the occasional Hawaiian monk seal. The snorkeling here is particularly rewarding, as the reef provides a habitat for numerous species that can be observed up close.

For those interested in surfing and bodyboarding, the waves near Nukumoi Point offer more challenging conditions. The beach park is also a favored spot for stand-up paddleboarding and kayaking, providing plenty of options for water-based activities.

Poipu Beach Park is well-equipped with amenities that enhance the visitor experience. Facilities include picnic tables, barbecue grills, restrooms, showers, and ample parking. Lifeguards are on duty throughout the day, ensuring the safety of swimmers and beachgoers. Shaded areas and grassy lawns provide comfortable spots for picnics and relaxation, making it a great location for a family outing.

The park's scenic beauty and accessibility make it a popular spot for watching sunsets and observing wildlife. It's not uncommon to see Hawaiian monk seals resting on the beach, and during the winter months, humpback whales can often be spotted offshore.

Poipu Beach Park's combination of excellent facilities, diverse recreational opportunities, and stunning natural beauty make it a must-visit destination on Kauai's south shore.

19.   Kukui'ula Village Shopping Center

Kukui'ula Village Shopping Center, located in Poipu on Kauai's south shore, is a vibrant and upscale shopping and dining destination that blends luxury with a laid-back island vibe. Designed to resemble a traditional Hawaiian village, Kukui'ula offers a unique shopping experience set amidst beautifully landscaped gardens and scenic views.

The shopping center features a variety of high-end boutiques, local artisan shops, and specialty stores. Visitors can browse an array of fashion, jewelry, home goods, and gifts, many of which highlight local craftsmanship and Hawaiian culture. Whether you're looking for a stylish outfit, a unique piece of art, or a memorable souvenir, Kukui'ula has something to offer.

In addition to shopping, Kukui'ula Village is a culinary hub, boasting a range of dining options that cater to diverse tastes. The center is home to several acclaimed restaurants that offer everything from gourmet cuisine and fresh seafood to casual dining and local favorites. Many of the eateries emphasize farm-to-table dining, sourcing ingredients from local farms and markets to create delicious and sustainable dishes. Popular spots include Merriman's Fish House, known for its fresh seafood and elegant atmosphere, and the casual yet sophisticated Tortilla Republic, offering modern Mexican cuisine.

For those interested in wellness and relaxation, Kukui'ula Village includes spa services, fitness centers, and yoga studios, providing visitors with opportunities to unwind and rejuvenate. The serene environment and upscale amenities make it an ideal place to indulge in some self-care.

Kukui'ula Village also hosts a variety of events and activities throughout the year, enhancing its community atmosphere. These include weekly farmers' markets, where visitors can purchase fresh produce, local foods, and handmade crafts, as well as live music performances, art exhibits, and cultural demonstrations. These events create a lively and engaging environment, offering a deeper connection to the local community and culture.

The center's beautiful setting, with its lush landscaping and open-air design, adds to the overall experience. Visitors can enjoy leisurely strolls through the village, taking in the tropical surroundings and scenic vistas.

20.   Spouting Horn

Spouting Horn, located on the south shore of Kauai near Poipu, is one of the island's most dramatic and popular natural attractions. This unique blowhole, formed by an ancient lava tube, offers a spectacular display as waves forcefully push water through the tube, creating a powerful spout that can reach heights of up to 50 feet.

The phenomenon occurs when ocean waves crash into the coastline, entering the narrow lava tube and being compressed. The pressure builds up and forces the water through the small opening at the top, resulting in a high, geyser-like spray. The spout is accompanied by a distinctive hissing or roaring sound, adding to the dramatic effect. The sight and sound of Spouting Horn are mesmerizing and provide a captivating natural spectacle for visitors.

Spouting Horn is particularly impressive during high tide and rough sea conditions, when the waves are more powerful and the spouts reach their maximum height. Visitors can view the blowhole from a safe distance at the designated viewing area, which offers unobstructed views of the coastline and the blowhole. The surrounding rocky shoreline and lush greenery enhance the scenic beauty of the location.

The site is also steeped in Hawaiian legend. According to local folklore, Spouting Horn is believed to be the work of a giant lizard or dragon that once terrorized the area. The creature was trapped in the lava tube by a brave warrior, and its roars are said to be the sounds heard when the water spouts. This myth adds an element of mystique to the natural wonder.

In addition to its natural beauty, the area around Spouting Horn is a great spot for observing marine life. Sea turtles are often seen swimming in the waters nearby, and during the winter months, humpback whales can be spotted offshore. The adjacent picnic area provides a lovely setting for a leisurely meal while enjoying the coastal views.

The Spouting Horn Park also features a small marketplace where local vendors sell handcrafted souvenirs, jewelry, and Hawaiian crafts. This is a great place to pick up unique gifts and support local artisans.

Molokai

1.   Kalaupapa National Historical Park

Established in 1980, the park preserves the story of the Kalaupapa and Kalawao settlements, where individuals afflicted with Hansen's disease (leprosy) were forcibly isolated from 1866 to 1969. The park honors the lives and experiences of these individuals and their caregivers, including the renowned Saint Damien de Veuster and Saint Marianne Cope, who dedicated their lives to caring for the patients.

Kalaupapa's history is a poignant chapter in Hawaii's past. During the 19th century, Hansen's disease was a feared and misunderstood illness. In an attempt to control its spread, the Hawaiian government implemented a policy of forced isolation, exiling those diagnosed with the disease to the remote Kalaupapa Peninsula. The peninsula's rugged terrain and steep sea cliffs made it an effective natural quarantine site. Initially, conditions were harsh, with limited resources and medical care, but over time, the settlement grew into a self-sufficient community.

Saint Damien, a Belgian priest, arrived at Kalaupapa in 1873 and became a central figure in the community. He provided medical care, built infrastructure, and advocated for the residents, improving their quality of life significantly. His work continued until his death from Hansen's disease in 1889. Saint Marianne Cope, a German-born American nun, arrived in 1883 and expanded upon Father Damien's efforts. She established a hospital and implemented modern healthcare practices, greatly enhancing the residents' well-being. Both were canonized by the Catholic Church for their compassionate service.

Visiting Kalaupapa National Historical Park is a unique and moving experience. The park is accessible only by plane, mule ride, or a challenging hike down a steep, 1,700-foot sea cliff, reflecting its historical isolation. The park offers guided tours that provide insights into the daily lives of the residents, the medical treatments they received, and the community they built.

2.   Halawa Valley

Halawa Valley, situated on the eastern end of Molokai, Hawaii, is a lush, verdant valley rich in natural beauty and cultural heritage. It is one of the oldest continuously inhabited areas in Hawaii, with a history that dates back over 1,300 years. This stunning valley, framed by towering cliffs and cascading waterfalls, offers visitors a glimpse into traditional Hawaiian life and the island's ancient history.

The journey to Halawa Valley is itself an adventure, involving a scenic drive along the island's coastal highway. This route provides breathtaking views of Molokai's rugged coastline, turquoise waters, and the occasional humpback whale during migration season. Upon arrival in the valley, visitors are greeted by a landscape of dense rainforests, taro patches, and pristine beaches, all of which contribute to the valley's serene and untouched atmosphere.

One of the main attractions in Halawa Valley is its waterfalls, particularly Moaula and Hipuapua Falls. These spectacular waterfalls, especially after heavy rainfall, are surrounded by lush vegetation and provide a stunning backdrop for hikers. The hike to Moaula Falls is a popular activity, offering a moderately challenging trek through the valley's rich ecosystem. The trail passes through ancient taro fields and other significant cultural sites, providing a deep connection to the land and its history. Guided tours, often led by local residents and descendants of the valley's original inhabitants, offer invaluable insights into the valley's history, flora, and fauna.

Halawa Valley is also a living cultural landscape. The valley has been continuously cultivated for centuries, primarily for taro, a staple crop in traditional Hawaiian agriculture. Visitors can see ancient lo'i (taro patches) and other remnants of early Hawaiian agricultural practices. These traditional farming methods have been preserved and are still practiced today, providing a direct link to the past.

The cultural significance of Halawa Valley extends beyond agriculture. The valley is home to several heiau (ancient Hawaiian temples) and other archaeological sites that offer insights into the religious and social practices of its early inhabitants. These sites are revered and protected, and visitors are encouraged to learn about and respect their cultural importance.

3.   Kapuaiwa Coconut Grove

Kapuaiwa Coconut Grove, located near the town of Kaunakakai on Molokai's south shore, is a historic and visually striking landmark. This ancient coconut grove, planted in the 1860s during the reign of King Kamehameha V, originally contained around 1,000 coconut palms, making it one of the largest and oldest coconut groves in Hawaii. Named in honor of King Kamehameha V, whose Hawaiian name was Lot Kapuaiwa, the grove stands as a testament to the island's royal history and the significance of the coconut palm in Hawaiian culture.

The grove's towering coconut palms, with their slender trunks and swaying fronds, create a picturesque and serene environment. The sight of these majestic trees silhouetted against the sky is particularly enchanting, especially at sunset when the colors of the sky enhance the natural beauty of the scene. The grove's proximity to the ocean adds to its appeal, with the gentle sound of waves providing a soothing backdrop to the rustling of palm leaves.

While the grove itself is not open to the public for safety reasons—falling coconuts and palm fronds pose a hazard—visitors can admire its beauty from nearby vantage points. There are several spots around the grove where visitors can take in the view and capture photographs of this iconic site. The area around the grove is also home to other historical sites, including the nearby Kaunakakai Wharf and the historic town of Kaunakakai, offering visitors additional points of interest to explore.

Kapuaiwa Coconut Grove is not only a place of historical significance but also a symbol of cultural heritage. The coconut palm, or niu in Hawaiian, has long been an important resource in Hawaiian culture. Every part of the tree is utilized, from the fruit, which provides food and drink, to the leaves, which are used for weaving baskets and mats. The trunks are used in construction, and the fibers can be made into ropes and other materials. The grove, therefore, represents the sustainable use of natural resources and the ingenuity of the Hawaiian people.

The grove's historical significance is further underscored by its connection to King Kamehameha V, a monarch known for his efforts to preserve Hawaiian traditions and culture during a time of significant change. His decision to plant the grove reflects his commitment to maintaining the island's natural beauty and cultural heritage.

4.   Kamakou Preserve

Kamakou Preserve, located in the mountainous interior of Molokai, is a pristine 2,774-acre nature reserve that protects one of Hawaii's most diverse and ecologically significant rainforests. Managed by The Nature Conservancy, the preserve is home to a remarkable array of endemic plants and animals, many of which are found nowhere else in the world. The preserve's rich biodiversity and pristine landscapes make it a vital area for conservation and a fascinating destination for nature enthusiasts.

Situated on the slopes of Kamakou, Molokai's highest peak, the preserve features a variety of ecosystems, including wet forests, bogs, and montane shrublands. This diversity of habitats supports over 200 species of plants, more than 40 of which are endemic to Molokai. Notable among these are the rare and endangered species such as the Molokai greenhood orchid, the Molokai ihi, and the Hawaiian damselfly. The preservation of these unique species is a primary focus of the conservation efforts at Kamakou.

Guided hikes offered by The Nature Conservancy provide a unique opportunity to explore the preserve's rich biodiversity. The most popular trail, the Pepeopae Bog Trail, leads hikers through lush forests of ohia and koa trees, across boardwalks that protect the delicate bog environment, and to scenic viewpoints overlooking Molokai's verdant valleys and rugged coastline. This trail offers hikers a chance to experience the diverse plant life and stunning natural beauty of Kamakou Preserve.

Birdwatchers will find Kamakou Preserve particularly rewarding, as it is a sanctuary for several native Hawaiian bird species. These include the endangered akikiki (Hawaiian creeper) and the Maui parrotbill, both of which are rare and difficult to spot elsewhere. The preserve's varied habitats also support other native birds such as the Hawaiian honeycreepers, whose colorful plumage and unique songs add to the enchanting atmosphere of the rainforest.

In addition to its ecological significance, Kamakou Preserve plays a crucial role in the conservation of Hawaii's natural heritage. Efforts to control invasive species, restore native vegetation, and protect endangered species are ongoing, ensuring that this vital ecosystem remains intact for future generations.

5.   Papohaku Beach Park

Papohaku Beach Park, located on the west end of Molokai, is one of the largest and most beautiful beaches in Hawaii. Stretching nearly three miles long and 100 yards wide, this expansive white sand beach offers a serene and unspoiled retreat for visitors seeking tranquility, natural beauty, and outdoor recreation. Papohaku's vast, open spaces and pristine environment make it a perfect destination for those looking to escape the crowds and enjoy a more peaceful beach experience.

The soft, golden sands of Papohaku Beach are ideal for sunbathing, beachcombing, and leisurely walks along the shore. The beach's size and relative isolation mean that it is often uncrowded, providing plenty of space for relaxation and solitude. The gentle slope of the beach into the ocean creates a beautiful, expansive shoreline that is perfect for enjoying the sun and sea breeze.

The clear waters of Papohaku Beach are suitable for swimming, although visitors should be cautious of strong currents, especially during the winter months when the surf can be rough. Lifeguards are not present at the beach, so it is important to exercise caution and be aware of ocean conditions. For those who prefer more active pursuits, the beach offers excellent opportunities for bodyboarding, surfing, and paddleboarding.

Papohaku Beach Park is also a great place for camping, with facilities that include picnic tables, restrooms, and showers. The park's spacious grounds and scenic ocean views make it a popular spot for weekend getaways and family outings. Camping permits are required and can be obtained from the local authorities, allowing visitors to fully immerse themselves in the natural beauty of the area.

One of the highlights of Papohaku Beach is its spectacular sunsets. The beach's western orientation provides an unobstructed view of the horizon, making it a perfect spot to watch the sun dip below the ocean. The vibrant colors of the sunset, combined with the expansive sky and tranquil setting, create a memorable and picturesque experience.

Lanai

1.   Polihua Beach

Polihua Beach, located on the northwest coast of Lanai, is a remote and pristine beach known for its stunning natural beauty and tranquil atmosphere. Stretching two miles along the coastline, Polihua Beach is the longest white-sand beach on the island. Despite its breathtaking scenery, it remains relatively untouched by tourism due to its secluded location and challenging access.

The beach is characterized by its expansive stretch of soft, golden sand and the stunning views it offers of the neighboring island of Molokai. The clear, blue waters of the Pacific Ocean add to the picturesque setting, creating an ideal backdrop for photography and quiet reflection. The isolation of Polihua Beach makes it a perfect destination for those seeking solitude and a break from the hustle and bustle of more crowded beaches.

Accessing Polihua Beach requires a bit of an adventure. The beach is reached via a rugged, unpaved road that is best navigated with a four-wheel-drive vehicle. This journey through the rugged terrain adds to the sense of adventure and discovery, rewarding visitors with the serene beauty of the beach upon arrival. The remote location means that amenities are non-existent, so visitors should come prepared with ample water, food, and sun protection.

Swimming at Polihua Beach is not recommended due to strong currents and high surf, especially during the winter months. The powerful waves and undertow can make the waters dangerous even for experienced swimmers. However, the beach is perfect for long walks, sunbathing, beachcombing, and picnicking. Wildlife enthusiasts may also spot green sea turtles and Hawaiian monk seals basking on the shore, as well as humpback whales breaching offshore during the winter migration season.

2.   Shipwreck Beach

Shipwreck Beach, located on the northeastern coast of Lanai, is an eight-mile-long stretch of rugged coastline famous for its historical shipwrecks and panoramic views. The beach is named for the various ships that have run aground on its coral reefs over the years, with the most prominent being a World War II-era Liberty Ship that still rests offshore.

The beach is characterized by its rocky shoreline, golden sand, and the striking image of the rusting shipwreck in the distance. The sight of the decaying vessel adds an element of intrigue and historical significance to the natural beauty of the area. The surrounding waters are notoriously rough and hazardous due to strong currents and a shallow reef, making the beach a graveyard for many ships over the centuries.

Accessing Shipwreck Beach involves a scenic drive along an unpaved, often bumpy road that requires a four-wheel-drive vehicle. The journey itself offers stunning views of Lanai's diverse landscapes, including dry grasslands and coastal scrub. Upon reaching the beach, visitors are greeted by a vast, untouched shoreline that invites exploration and contemplation.

While swimming is not advisable due to the treacherous waters, Shipwreck Beach is ideal for beachcombing, picnicking, and hiking. The area is rich in marine life, and beachgoers can often spot sea turtles, seabirds, and occasionally, Hawaiian monk seals. The beach is also a fantastic location for photography, with the rusting shipwreck providing a dramatic focal point against the backdrop of the ocean and sky.

Shipwreck Beach holds cultural and historical significance for Lanai. The Liberty Ship, which dates back to the 1940s, serves as a reminder of the island's connection to World War II history. Additionally, the beach was historically a site for traditional Hawaiian fishing and gathering, adding layers of cultural heritage to its appeal.

For those interested in exploring further, the beach is part of a larger coastal trail that leads to other points of interest, including the remains of ancient Hawaiian villages and petroglyphs. This trail offers a glimpse into the island's rich cultural history and natural beauty.

3.   Keahiakawelo (Garden of the Gods)

Keahiakawelo, also known as the Garden of the Gods, is a striking and otherworldly landscape located on the northwestern end of Lanai. This unique geological wonder is characterized by its surreal rock formations, vibrant red and orange hues, and expansive views, creating a stark contrast to the lush, tropical environments typically associated with Hawaii.

The name Keahiakawelo translates to "the fire of Kawelo," and the area is steeped in Hawaiian legend. According to local lore, the rock garden was created by the powerful kahuna (priest) Kawelo, who set a fire to produce the landscape's distinctive colors and formations. The site's mystical atmosphere and historical significance add an intriguing cultural layer to its natural beauty.

Accessing Keahiakawelo involves a drive along a rugged, unpaved road that winds through Lanai's arid interior. A four-wheel-drive vehicle is necessary to navigate the challenging terrain, but the journey is part of the adventure. The road to the Garden of the Gods offers scenic views of Lanai's diverse landscapes, from dry grasslands to rocky outcrops.

Upon arrival, visitors are greeted by a landscape that feels almost Martian in its appearance. The rock formations, sculpted by centuries of wind erosion, create a labyrinth of spires, buttes, and boulders. The iron-rich soil lends the rocks their vibrant red and orange colors, which glow even more intensely at sunrise and sunset. The panoramic views from Keahiakawelo stretch across the island and out to the Pacific Ocean, with the islands of Molokai and Maui visible in the distance on clear days.

Keahiakawelo is a haven for photographers and nature enthusiasts. The unique rock formations and dramatic lighting conditions offer endless opportunities for capturing stunning images. The area is also a fantastic spot for quiet contemplation and appreciating the raw, untamed beauty of Lanai's landscape.

The Garden of the Gods is more than just a visual spectacle; it is also a place of spiritual significance. The site is considered sacred by Native Hawaiians, and visitors are encouraged to respect the area by staying on designated paths and not disturbing the rock formations.

4.   Munro Trail

The Munro Trail, located on the island of Lanai, offers an adventurous and scenic journey through some of the island's most diverse landscapes. This 12.8-mile trail, named after George Munro, a New Zealand forestry expert who worked on Lanai in the early 20th century, provides hikers and off-road enthusiasts with breathtaking views, lush vegetation, and a glimpse into the island's natural history.

The trail begins near the Lanai City and winds its way up to the summit of Lanaihale, the highest point on the island at 3,370 feet. The ascent offers a gradual change in scenery, starting from the arid lowlands and progressing through dense pine forests and verdant uplands. The trail is renowned for its diversity of plant life, including native Hawaiian species and introduced pine trees planted by Munro to help combat soil erosion and increase rainfall on the island.

One of the highlights of the Munro Trail is the panoramic views it offers. As hikers or drivers make their way along the trail, they are treated to stunning vistas of Lanai's coastline, neighboring islands, and the vast Pacific Ocean. On clear days, it is possible to see the islands of Maui, Molokai, Oahu, and even the Big Island in the distance. These viewpoints provide excellent opportunities for photography and moments of reflection.

The trail is accessible to both hikers and four-wheel-drive vehicles, although the rugged terrain can be challenging. The narrow, winding path requires careful navigation, especially after rain when the trail can become muddy and slippery. Despite these challenges, the journey is incredibly rewarding, offering a sense of adventure and the chance to experience Lanai's natural beauty up close.

The Munro Trail also holds ecological significance. The reforestation efforts initiated by George Munro have created a unique environment where native and introduced species coexist. The pine forests attract various bird species, including native Hawaiian birds like the apapane and amakihi, making it a great spot for birdwatching. The trail's diverse habitats also support a range of other wildlife, adding to the richness of the experience.

5.   Lanai Culture & Heritage Center

The Lanai Culture & Heritage Center, located in Lanai City, is a vital institution dedicated to preserving and sharing the rich cultural and historical heritage of the island of Lanai. Established in 2007, the center provides visitors with an in-depth understanding of Lanai's unique history, from its early Hawaiian settlement to its development as a pineapple plantation and beyond.

The museum's exhibits cover a wide range of topics, including the island's geological formation, ancient Hawaiian culture, and the impact of the plantation era. Artifacts on display include traditional Hawaiian tools, weapons, and everyday items, as well as photographs, documents, and memorabilia from the pineapple plantation period. These exhibits provide a comprehensive overview of the island's diverse history and the people who have shaped its development.

One of the center's primary missions is to preserve the stories and traditions of Lanai's Native Hawaiian community. The center offers educational programs, workshops, and cultural events that highlight traditional practices such as hula, lei-making, and taro cultivation. These programs aim to foster a deeper understanding and appreciation of Hawaiian culture among both residents and visitors.

In addition to its permanent exhibits, the Lanai Culture & Heritage Center hosts rotating exhibits that explore various aspects of the island's history and culture. These temporary exhibits often feature the work of local artists and craftspeople, providing a platform for contemporary cultural expression.

The center also plays an active role in the preservation of Lanai's historical sites. Working in collaboration with local organizations and government agencies, the center supports efforts to protect and restore significant cultural landmarks, such as the Kaunolu Village Site and the Keahiakawelo (Garden of the Gods). These preservation initiatives help ensure that Lanai's rich cultural heritage is maintained for future generations.

6.   Lanai Cat Sanctuary

The Lanai Cat Sanctuary, located on the island of Lanai, is a haven for cats and cat lovers alike. Established in 2009, the sanctuary provides a safe and nurturing environment for more than 600 cats, many of whom are rescued strays or feral cats from around the island. The sanctuary's mission is to protect the island's native bird populations while also caring for the feline residents, creating a unique and compassionate solution to the challenges posed by feral cat populations.

The sanctuary is situated on a spacious outdoor property, providing the cats with ample room to roam, play, and interact with visitors. The environment is designed to be both stimulating and comfortable for the cats, with plenty of shaded areas, climbing structures, and cozy spots for napping. Visitors to the sanctuary are greeted by friendly cats eager for attention and affection, making it a delightful destination for animal lovers.

One of the sanctuary's primary goals is to reduce the impact of feral cats on Lanai's native bird species, many of which are endangered. By providing a dedicated space for these cats, the sanctuary helps to protect vulnerable bird populations from predation. This dual focus on animal welfare and environmental conservation makes the Lanai Cat Sanctuary a model for humane and effective wildlife management.

The sanctuary is open to the public, offering free admission and welcoming visitors of all ages. Guests can spend time interacting with the cats, learning about the sanctuary's work, and even adopting a cat if they wish to provide a permanent home for one of the residents. The staff at the sanctuary are passionate about animal care and are happy to share their knowledge and experiences with visitors.

In addition to its direct care for the cats, the Lanai Cat Sanctuary engages in community outreach and education. The organization works to promote responsible pet ownership, including spaying and neutering programs, to prevent the growth of feral cat populations. They also collaborate with other animal welfare organizations to advocate for humane treatment of animals and environmental conservation efforts.

7.   Kaunolu Village Site

The Kaunolu Village Site, located on the southern coast of Lanai, is one of the most significant archaeological and historical sites in Hawaii. Once a thriving fishing village, Kaunolu was an important cultural and political center for Native Hawaiians and served as a retreat for Hawaiian royalty, including King Kamehameha I. The site offers a fascinating glimpse into the traditional Hawaiian way of life and is a valuable link to the island's past.

Kaunolu Village Site is situated on a scenic bluff overlooking Kaunolu Bay, providing stunning views of the ocean and surrounding landscape. The site covers approximately 22 acres and includes a wealth of archaeological features, such as house platforms, heiau (temples), petroglyphs, and fishing shrines. These remnants provide a vivid picture of daily life in an ancient Hawaiian village, including social, religious, and economic activities.

One of the most notable features of Kaunolu is the Halulu Heiau, a large and well-preserved temple complex. This heiau was used for religious ceremonies and is believed to have been dedicated to the Hawaiian god of war, Ku. The site also includes a sacred sacrificial stone and other religious artifacts, highlighting the spiritual significance of the area.

Another key attraction at Kaunolu is the petroglyphs, ancient rock carvings that depict various aspects of Hawaiian life, including human figures, animals, and symbolic patterns. These petroglyphs are an important cultural treasure, providing insights into the beliefs, practices, and artistic expressions of the island's early inhabitants.

Kaunolu Village Site is also known for its association with King Kamehameha I, who used the village as a royal retreat in the late 18th and early 19th centuries. The area served as a strategic location for planning military campaigns and consolidating his power over the Hawaiian Islands.

Visitors to Kaunolu Village Site can explore the area through self-guided tours, although guided tours are available and highly recommended for a deeper understanding of the site's historical and cultural significance. Interpretive signs and plaques provide valuable information about the various features and their roles in traditional Hawaiian society.

8.   Hulopoe Bay

Hulopoe Bay, located on the southern coast of Lanai, is one of the island's most beautiful and popular destinations. Known for its crystal-clear waters, vibrant marine life, and pristine white-sand beach, Hulopoe Bay offers a perfect setting for a variety of outdoor activities, making it a favorite spot for both relaxation and adventure.

The bay is part of the Hulopoe Marine Life Conservation District, established to protect the area's rich marine biodiversity. As a result, the waters of Hulopoe Bay are teeming with colorful fish, coral reefs, and other marine life, making it an excellent location for snorkeling and diving. Visitors can explore the underwater world and encounter species such as butterflyfish, parrotfish, and even the occasional sea turtle or dolphin.

The beach at Hulopoe Bay is equally inviting, with its soft, white sand and gently sloping shore. The calm, clear waters provide ideal conditions for swimming, and the beach is well-maintained with facilities such as restrooms, showers, picnic tables, and barbecue grills. Lifeguards are on duty, ensuring a safe and enjoyable experience for visitors of all ages.

One of the highlights of Hulopoe Bay is its tide pools, located on the eastern side of the beach. These natural pools, formed by volcanic rock, are filled with a variety of marine creatures, including small fish, sea urchins, and starfish. Exploring the tide pools is a popular activity, especially for families with children, offering an educational and interactive way to learn about the local marine ecosystem.

Hulopoe Bay is also renowned for its scenic beauty. The surrounding cliffs and rocky outcrops provide a stunning backdrop to the turquoise waters, creating a picturesque setting that is perfect for photography and simply soaking in the natural surroundings. The bay's west-facing orientation makes it an excellent spot to watch the sunset, with the sky painted in vibrant hues as the sun dips below the horizon.

Adjacent to Hulopoe Bay is the luxurious Four Seasons Resort Lanai, which offers world-class amenities and services. While the beach is open to the public, resort guests have access to additional facilities, including beachside dining and water sports equipment rentals.

9. Pu'Upehe Islet Seabird Sanctuary

Pu'Upehe Islet, also known as Sweetheart Rock, is a small but striking islet located just off the southern coast of Lanai near Hulopoe Bay. This picturesque rock formation is not only a scenic landmark but also a vital seabird sanctuary, providing a safe nesting habitat for several species of seabirds. The islet's natural beauty and ecological significance make it an important destination for visitors to Lanai.

The islet rises dramatically from the ocean, reaching a height of approximately 80 feet. Its sheer cliffs and rugged terrain create an imposing yet beautiful silhouette against the backdrop of the blue Pacific. The striking appearance of Pu'Upehe Islet, combined with its isolation and inaccessibility, has made it a symbol of natural beauty and mystery.

Pu'Upehe Islet is named after a tragic Hawaiian legend. According to the story, a young woman named Pu'Upehe was so beautiful that her lover, Makakehau, hid her in a sea cave to protect her from other suitors. One day, while Makakehau was away, a powerful storm surged, drowning Pu'Upehe in the cave. In his grief, Makakehau climbed the rock and buried her at the summit before leaping to his death. This poignant tale adds a layer of cultural and emotional depth to the islet's allure.

The islet serves as an important sanctuary for seabirds, providing a safe and undisturbed nesting site. Species such as the wedge-tailed shearwater and the brown booby are known to breed on Pu'Upehe Islet. The rugged cliffs and isolation from predators make it an ideal location for these birds to raise their young. The sanctuary status of the islet helps protect these vulnerable species and ensures the preservation of their critical nesting habitat.

Visitors to Hulopoe Bay can enjoy stunning views of Pu'Upehe Islet from the shore or take a short hike to a vantage point on the cliffs overlooking the islet. The hike offers panoramic views of the coastline and the ocean, making it a popular spot for photography and contemplation. The clear waters around the islet are also a great place for snorkeling and kayaking, allowing visitors to appreciate the marine life and the islet's striking presence from the water.

Made in United States
Orlando, FL
04 December 2024

54942190R10070